D1193875

MORTE D'AUTHOR
An Autopsy

The Arts and Their Philosophies
a series edited by Joseph Margolis

Morte d'Author

An Autopsy

H. L. Hix

Temple University Press

PHILADELPHIA

Temple University Press, Philadelphia 19122
Copyright © 1990 by Temple University. All rights reserved
Published 1990
Printed in the United States of America

The paper used in this publication meets the minimum
requirements of American National Standard for Information
Sciences—Permanence of Paper for Printed Library Materials,
ANSI Z39.48-1984 ∞

Library of Congress Cataloging-in-Publication Data
Hix, H. L.
    Morte d'author : an autopsy / H. L. Hix.
        p.   cm. — (The Arts and their philosophies)
    Contents: Includes bibliographical references.
    ISBN 0-87722-734-9 (alk. paper)
    1. Literature—Philosophy. 2. Authorship—Philosophy.
3. Creation (Literary, artistic, etc.) I. Title. II. Series.
PN49.H58 1990
801—DC20   90-32657
                                                    CIP

Contents

Acknowledgments

As is only fitting for an examination of the alleged "death of the author," I am left with the impression that this book has written itself. At no time during its genesis did I feel that I was exerting any influence over its content; always I felt two steps behind. Nor does it seem less alien to me now. During the last five years, I have considered other writing projects more personally important, yet this one alone is complete, as if by a will of its own.

This text's following its own will rather than mine has not kept me from incurring debts to many people during its writing, notably Gene Fendt, Kathy Higgins, Brent Spencer, Paul Woodruff, Ramón Saldívar, and R. J. Kaufmann. My wife, Sheila Pedigo, has supported and encouraged me from the project's inception. And, more directly than anyone else, Drs. Lynne McFall and Louis Mackey have been friends, foes, advisors, and critics from the beginning; they do not know the extent of my gratitude to them or my respect for them.

For the generosity of their assessment of the book and for their valuable advice concerning revisions, I want to thank Joseph Margolis and two anonymous readers for Temple University Press. I am especially grateful to Jane Cullen for her advocacy and expertise.

Earlier versions of portions of this book have previously appeared in the *Iowa Review* and *Notes on Contemporary Literature*.

Credits

MORTE D'AUTHOR

An Autopsy

CHAPTER I

Vital Signs

In 1968 Roland Barthes proclaimed the death of the author. Like Nietzsche's proclamation of the death of God, Barthes's proclamation is not a literal statement. "The death of the author" is the vehicle of a metaphor whose tenor is, roughly, that there is no transcendent figure at the origin of a text's meaning. Yet, for all their similarity of manner, the two proclamations are radically different in nature. If Nietzsche's proclamation is an obituary, Barthes's is a suicide note, and an enigmatic one at that, for "this enemy of authors is himself preeminently an author, a writer whose varied products reveal a personal style and vision" (Culler 1983, 11). And what is worse than the fact that Barthes, himself an author, proclaimed the death of the author is that he proclaimed it in writing. There have been numerous direct and indirect responses to Barthes's essay, some in the form of additions to or modifications of Barthes's view, others in the form of arguments contending that reports of the author's death have been greatly exaggerated. In the face of this conflicting testimony, an autopsy is called for. This book will be an autopsy in both of Webster's senses of the word: "(1) an examination and dissection of a dead body, esp. by a coroner, to discover the cause of death, damage done by a disease, etc.; post-mortem; (2) a detailed critical analysis of a book, play, etc., or of some event."[1] I will offer an analysis of several texts centered on the event of the author's death in an attempt to show that none of the author's previous examiners has been careful to establish positive identification of the body, and I will examine and dissect the author's body to see what has become of its vital signs and what (so to speak) remains.

One thing about which almost all involved in the debate about the author agree is that the author is a modern figure. For example, Barthes, Michel Foucault, and Alexander Nehamas all date the author's birth at about the time of Hobbes,[2] making him a logical starting point for this study. Even for an autopsy, a nativity, no matter how unnatural, is not a bad place to begin.

In chapter 16 of *Leviathan*, Hobbes places "authors" in the larger class of "persons." The larger class he defines in this way: "*A Person, is he whose words or actions are considered, either as his own, or as representing the words or actions of an other man, or of any other thing to whom they are attributed, whether Truly or by Fiction*" (1984, 217). From that definition alone, it is not obvious where Hobbes is headed, but his direction becomes clear in the next sentence, where he divides the class of persons into two subclasses: "When [his words or actions] are considered as his owne, then is he called a *Naturall Person:* And when they are considered as representing the words and actions of an other, then is he a *Feigned* or *Artificiall person*." The difference between the classes has to do with ownership and property rights: Natural persons own their actions, artificial persons only rent them.

In addition to being a subclass of the category "persons," the author is also a member of the pair author/actor. An author is a natural person; an actor is an artificial person, and the author's tenant. The author/actor pair has to do with citizenship: To be an author or an actor entails certain rights and obligations, and a "special kind of relationship" (Kronman 1980, 161) with the other member of the pair. Hobbes's example action is the making of a covenant. When an actor makes a covenant, he appeals to his right to represent someone else: "By Authority, is always understood a Right of doing any act" (Hobbes 1984, 218). And his action entails obligation for the author: "When the Actor maketh a Covenant by Authority, he bindeth thereby the Author, no lesse than if he had made it himselfe" (218). It follows that "the right of an actor and the obligation of his author are correlative notions: each entails the other" (Kronman 1980, 162). So Hobbes's view is this:

> Of Persons Artificiall, some have their words and actions *Owned* by those whom they represent. And the Person is the *Actor;* and he that owneth his words and actions, is the AUTHOR: In which case the Actor acteth by Authority. For that which in speaking of goods and possessions, is called an *Owner,* and in latine *Dominus,* in Greek [*kyrios*]; speaking of Actions, is called Author. And as the Right of possession, is called Dominion; so the Right of doing any Action, is called AUTHORITY. (218)

Nehamas says "it is easy to see" that this passage applies to literary authors as well (1987, 267), but Nehamas's opinion notwithstanding, this passage's applicability to literary authors is not self-evident. Hobbes talks about authors and authority in the context of the process of contract making, which he sees as the foundation of the commonwealth. An actor is one who is empowered to make a covenant for which the author whom he represents will assume responsibility. An actor is empowered to do only what his author wishes or commands; yet this inequality is voluntary, and is therefore made possible by a prior equality that Anthony Kronman calls "contractual capacity" (1980, 170). Contractual capacity, the ability to enter into voluntary contracts (like the one between author and actor), entails the ability "to participate in the foundation of the common-wealth" (Kronman 1980, 170). Everyone, even an actor, is an author. Not all of this appears to be true of literary authors: Their actors (their texts) are not also authors, and have not entered into a contract with them voluntarily; it is not clear that texts can utter words and perform actions owned by their authors in the same way as can the "persons artificiall" Hobbes talks about; and so on.

Recent challenges to the notion of the author derived histori-cally from Hobbes (challenges like Barthes's "The Death of the Author"), in their attempt to show the *dis*analogy between literary authors and Hobbes's "Author," aim at the issue of ownership. And there are many disturbing questions. What does it mean to own one's actions? It may entail accepting responsibility for them, but it may not entail determining their meaning, their consequences, or their effects. What sort of privi-leges does ownership entail? Not a strict autonomy: The owner of a Ferrari has the right to spray paint it, but not to run over pedestrians with it; and the owner of a van Gogh has the right to hang it in her upstairs bathroom, but not to spray paint it. The author's ownership of the text has usually been taken to mean that he has the right to determine its meaning, but Barthes and others have questioned both whether the author is the text's owner at all and whether he has the right to determine its meaning.

My concern in this book, however, will be not primarily with the assumption that authors own their texts, but with an assumption that I believe both sides, the traditional pro–authorial-ownership side and the trendy anti–authorial-owner-ship side, share: what I will call the assumption of homogeneity. According to this assumption, the author, whether she is a historical individual or a character in the text, whether she is or is not the owner of the text, is singular and unitary.

Here is the problem. If a straw poll were conducted today in the faculty lounges and classrooms of university philosophy departments, the statement "Descartes is the founder of modern philosophy" would receive approbation from all but a few who suspect treachery, a few mavericks, and a few students flunking their "Intro" classes. Yet in spite of the almost universal agreement about the statement's truth, it is not clear what the statement means. It can hardly refer to the historical person who lived from 1596 to 1650, attended La Flèche, and maintained for some time a correspondence with Princess Elizabeth; that person is dead, and would be more properly referred to by using the past tense. If the historical person René Descartes is meant, the statement should read "Descartes was the founder of modern philosophy" or "Descartes founded modern philosophy." Perhaps the name "Descartes" refers in this use to the works written by the historical person, rather than to the historical person himself. However, if that is so, the use of the word "founder" seems mistaken, since it apparently implies an intentional agent who by an action(s) at a given time initiates an institution that is temporally posterior to that action, and we are not accustomed to thinking of books in that way. Books do not found institutions by initiating a temporal sequence and then disappearing, like some Johnny Appleseed of the mind; they persist and remain active in the institution itself, so that if a book can be said to found anything it is in a manner more like a seed than a sower. If by "Descartes" the texts composed by the historical person are meant, rather than the person himself, the statement should read "Descartes is the foundation of modern philosophy."

Apparently the statement "Descartes is the founder of modern philosophy," if it is to be sensible, must refer to something that fits the definite description, "the author of certain important philosophical texts, notably the *Discourse on Method* and

7

Meditations on First Philosophy." But that, of course, raises more questions than it answers. If "Descartes the author" is not the same as "Descartes the person," then what is the relationship between the two? Is it simply the mutual historical connection to "Descartes the person" that allows us to speak of the *Discourse* and the *Meditations* as being by the same "Descartes the author"? Or is it that they somehow project the same author? If so, what makes their author the same author in spite of the obvious differences between the two works? What about the *Dioptrics* and *Meteors*? Do they have the same author as the *Discourse,* in spite of their being scientific works, not philosophical works? Is "Descartes the mathematician" the same as "Descartes the author"? The questions could go on, but they all add up to one question: Just what *is* an author?

Attention to that question has grown in this century, and blossomed recently. But it will not bear fruit until the assumption of homogeneity is discarded. A resolution to the set of problems revolving around the "Descartes the person vs. Descartes the author" dilemma will not be possible until that set of problems is approached at the same time as the set of problems revolving around the simple observation that when one says "Homer is the author of the *Odyssey,*" the subject to which one refers ("Homer") is very different from the subject to which one refers when one says "Thomas Pynchon is the author of *Gravity's Rainbow,*" and stands in a different relation to the text he is said to be author of; and the same is true for the propositions "Parmenides is the author of a number of fragments" and "Luke is the author of the third Gospel." There was no single historical individual named Homer who by himself composed an epic called the *Odyssey,* but there is a living individual born in 1937 who by himself wrote a novel called *Gravity's Rainbow.* There was a historical individual named Parmenides with whom a number of fragments are associated, but how closely the fragments, which have come to us through intermediaries, approximate what the historical individual wrote is a topic of debate; and there was a historical individual named Luke who probably wrote down the Gospel attributed to him, but whether he or God is the source of its content is a topic of debate.

The problem, in other words, is that the questions all recent critics (from Wimsatt and Beardsley to Foucault and Derrida) have tried to answer about the author, namely, whether he is the same as the historical writer and whether he has control over the meaning of the text, will not be answered until serious notice is given to the fact that our term "author" does not describe a single function, but covers an array of functions that in the case of a given text need not be, and often are not, performed by a single individual. When someone speaks of God as the author of the Bible, of Moses as the author of the Pentateuch, of Johannes Climacus as the author of *Concluding Unscientific Postscript*, or of Shakespeare as the author of the major tragedies, she means something different by "author" each time. God might be thought of by believers as having written the Bible, but only in the sense of having "inspired" a number of men to write its parts, so that God would be viewed as the motivating and unifying force behind the text. But the same believer who calls God the author of the Bible might also call Moses the author of the Pentateuch, if by "author" she means Moses as the human instrument whom God inspired (whether or not she thinks of this Moses as identical with the character Moses in the account of the Exodus). The book of Genesis might be legitimately described by individuals with certain theological beliefs as having numerous authors, then: God, the inspiration for their content and the source of their authority; Moses, the human leader under whose name Genesis is linked with Exodus, Leviticus, Numbers, and Deuteronomy; the oral tradition(s) in which Genesis has its roots; and the long chain of priests, scribes, and scholars responsible for composing, compiling, and preserving the text. Johannes Climacus, by contrast, is a wholly fictional character who, since he does not exist "in reality," could never actually have written anything. Still, he is listed on the title page and referred to in Kierkegaardian scholarship as the author of the *Postscript*. He functions, not as a unifying force like God the author of the Bible, but as a separating force, isolating one group of works written by S. Kierkegaard from others. The Bible makes claims of unity (or at least has such claims made for it), in spite of its historical connection to countless "authors"; *Concluding Unscientific Postscript* claims to be isolated from works by Johannes de Silentio, Constantin Constantius, Anti-Climacus, and others, in spite of their mutual connection to a single individual, Søren Kierkegaard. Shakespeare as the author of the tragedies might function in any number of ways: as a reference to the historical person who wrote those works, as the "author-figure" projected by the tragedies (as distinct from the figure projected by the comedies), as a "standard" by which to test spurious works, and so on. Many other examples could be given (and will be given in later chapters) to illustrate the wide variety of meanings common usage demands of the term "author," yet criticism has until now not offered a picture of the author that is capable of incorporating all the meanings usage demands. I try in what follows to supply such a picture, and to make possible thereby the progress of the study of authorship past the assumption of homogeneity, upon which so far it has foundered.

To accomplish its objective, the book is divided into four parts. In the first, "Six Characters in Search of an Author," I examine the major modern theories of authorship, attempting to show how each view, while it may suffice for a limited number of cases or as a means to a desired theoretical conclusion, is not comprehensive. I argue that, as a result of the assumption of homogeneity, each of the views considered mistakes one aspect of the author for the whole, either the author as origin/cause of the text or as function/effect of the text, and that a satisfactory view of authorship must recognize and integrate both of those aspects. Taking that shared failure of previous views as a signpost, the next two parts of the book are devoted to the two aspects respectively. In "The Creative Author," I consider the author as origin/cause of the text. As a first approach, I identify five different ways in which the writer's part in the creation of the text is thought of, with the aim of showing how ideas about the creative process itself entail commitments about what an author is by identifying the roles and responsibilities of the human agent(s) involved. As a second approach, I isolate forces that render creative acts unique, with the aim of showing the variety of the acts whose agents we refer to as authors. In "The Created Author," I consider the other aspect of the author: as function/effect of the text. First, I try to show that Wayne Booth's concept of the "implied author" is built on the assumption of homogeneity, and that texts can supply their readers with more than the one "implied author" Booth will permit. Second, I describe the three most important such "authors" and consider ways in which their interaction can affect the interpretation of a text. The final part of the book, "Post-Mortem," asks about the consequences of discarding the assumption of homogeneity, and begins to suggest applications for the two sets of constructs set out in the second and third parts of the book. First, I suggest that to deny the assumption of homogeneity, though it entails that the historical writer is not the exclusive locus of meaning, does not entail that meaning has no locus. Second, I argue that the denial of the assumption of homogeneity need not entail that one is no longer entitled to make aesthetic and ethical judgments about texts and writers.

I should also delimit the scope of this book. The interpretive question about the author is one of a set of related metaphysical, aesthetic, and ethical questions about the philosophical subject. While I recognize that the question of the author takes place within this larger context, this book will limit itself to discussion of the author. I am persuaded that any theory of interpretation that misunderstands what an author is cannot hope to understand what a text is and how it conveys—or produces or yields (q.e.d.)—meaning. The arguably more important point is that a theory of interpretation that misunderstands what an author is also misunderstands what a reader is, so that if there is any validity in the old Socratic ideal of self-knowledge, and if texts are valuable insofar as they serve that ideal, failure to understand the author is a flaw of some magnitude. First be reconciled to the author, and then come and offer thy theory. But while an understanding of the author is a necessary condition of an adequate theory of interpretation, it is not a sufficient condition. This book is only a series of steps toward an understanding of the author; it is not an entire theory of interpretation. Prolegomena to any future interpretation, perhaps, but not a critique. I hope that by restricting itself to the pursuit of a narrowly defined end, the book will provide, for an investigation that needs it, a good beginning.

ONE

Six Characters in Search of

an Author

Said Yo-Yo:
"What part ob yu iz deh poEM??"
—Ezra Pound

CHAPTER 2

Foucault and Nehamas

Of the many recent scholarly skirmishes (declared and undeclared) concerning the nature and status of the author, the two most extensive battles center on two different kinds of recognition. Michel Foucault and Alexander Nehamas argue over *how* one should recognize an author. Theirs is a question of *per*ception: What is an author? What does one look like? Roland Barthes and William Gass, on the other hand, argue over *whether* one should recognize an author. Theirs is a question of *re*ception: Should an author's presence be acknowledged? Does the author retain any authority over the meaning of his work? I will consider first the debate between Foucault and Nehamas.

Foucault asserts the need for a new set of questions about discourse, based on the "murmur of indifference" he cites from Beckett: "What matter who's speaking?" But such a murmur of indifference presupposes a new answer to the question "Who *is* speaking?," and Foucault claims to be giving (or at least paving the way for) such a new answer in his essay "What Is an Author?" Nehamas argues in two separate essays, one partially and the other primarily directed against Foucault, that the question regarding the author should be changed from "Who *is* speaking?" to "Who *can be* speaking?," and that the interpretation of a text should be guided by the "historically plausible" characterization of the author constructed by the reader in answer to that question. I propose a third alternative. I contend (with Foucault and against Nehamas) that the important question regarding the author *is* "Who is speaking?" but that both Foucault and Nehamas conflate that question with the question "Who has spoken?"; and I contend (against both) that neither the question "Who is speaking?" nor the question "Who has spoken?" is a matter of indifference to the reader.

Foucault begins his essay with an apology for his asking the "slightly odd question" "What is an author?" He says that, while his objective in *The Order of Things* was "to determine . . . the functional conditions of specific discursive practices" (1977, 114), he was criticized (rightly, he admits) for allowing the names of Buffon, Cuvier, Ricardo, Marx, and others to function ambiguously. Some of the questions resulting from this ambiguous usage Foucault claims to have dealt with in *The Archaeology of Knowledge*, but "as a privileged moment of individualization in the history of philosophy and science, the question of the author demands a more direct response" (115), which he will give in "What Is an Author?" Even "the question of the author," though, is not a single, simple issue (there are, for instance, numerous sociohistorical questions), so Foucault restricts himself "to the singular relationship that holds between an author and a text, the manner in which a text apparently points to this figure who is outside and precedes it" (115).

Of Beckett's "murmur of indifference," "What matter who's speaking?," Foucault claims that such indifference is "one of the fundamental ethical principles of contemporary writing" (116). This principle "dominates writing as an ongoing practice and slights our customary attention to the finished product"; and Foucault illustrates the principle by glances at two of its themes. The first is that "the writing of our day has freed itself from the necessity of 'expression'." It is "an interplay of signs,

16

regulated less by the content it signifies than by the very nature of the signifier." It is a game that leaves its own rules behind, something like Wittgenstein's ladder that is to be thrown away once one has climbed it. It is not, argues Foucault, a linguistic repository for the writer (as someone like Wordsworth would claim for his own writing); quite the contrary, "it is primarily concerned with creating an opening where the writing subject endlessly disappears" (116).

The second theme is the "more familiar" one of "the kinship between writing and death" (116). This theme inverts the older conception of narrative as a protection against death, which Foucault exemplifies by Greek epic ("which was designed to guarantee the immortality of a hero") and Arabic stories (such as the Arabian Nights, in which the narrative forestalls death). "Writing," Foucault claims, "is now linked to sacrifice and to the sacrifice of life itself; it is a voluntary obliteration of the self that does not require representation in books because it takes place in the everyday existence of the writer. Where a work had the duty of creating immortality, it now attains the right to kill, to become the murderer of its author" (117). For Foucault, then, the text functions in relation to the author in the same way that for Freud the "double" functions in relation to the individual. The passage just quoted is in fact almost the double of this passage from Freud:

> The 'double' was originally an insurance against the destruction of the ego, an 'energetic denial of the power of death', as Rank says; and probably the 'immortal' soul was the first 'double' of the body. . . . Such ideas, however, have sprung from the soil of unbounded self-love, from the primary narcissism which dominates the mind of the child and of primitive man. But when this stage has been surmounted, the 'double' reverses its aspect. From having

been an assurance of immortality, it becomes the uncanny harbinger of death. (1959e, 235)

For Freud the change in the conception of the "double" from guarantor of immortality to "harbinger of death" is one result of the abandonment of primary narcissism, either in the psychological development of the individual or in the cultural development of the species. Similarly, for Foucault the change in the conception of the text, the author's "double," from guarantor of immortality to murderer is a result of a philosophical shift, a cultural change, a development of writing.

But the consequences of this event, despite its familiarity to philosophy and criticism, have not been on Foucault's view "fully explored." Instead, certain problems "have merely served to arrest the possibility of genuine change [in critical practice]" (118); Foucault considers two of these problems. The first is that, although criticism has recognized that its task is not "to reconstitute an author's thought and experience through his work" but that instead the structures of a work should be studied "for their intrinsic and internal relationships" (118), there is no satisfactory theory "to encompass the questions generated by a work" (119). This problem is a practical one for an editor undertaking the publication of an author's complete works (Is this laundry bill a work? Why not?), and it is one Foucault discusses more extensively in *The Archaeology of Knowledge*. The second problem is "the notion of *écriture*" (119). This notion, Foucault says, is "a remarkably profound attempt to elaborate the conditions of any text," but as it has so far been employed it "has merely transposed the empirical characteristics of an author to a transcendental anonymity" (120). That is, the affirmations of the sacred origin of writing and "the religious principle of hidden meanings" are taken from the author by the concept of *écriture* and "reinscribe[d] in transcendental terms" as forgetfulness, repression, and so on. Thus the "conception of *écriture* sustains the privileges of the author through the safeguard of the a priori" (120).

Foucault's next question is: Given that the author has disappeared, what is the name of an author and how does it function? "The name of an author," he answers, citing Searle, "poses all the problems related to the category of the proper name" (121). The proper name "has other than indicative functions": First, it is to an extent a description. When a person uses the name "George Washington," he uses a name that means one or more definite descriptions: for example, "the first president of the United States," or "the man who wore wooden dentures." Second, a proper name "has other functions than that of signification": To learn that George Washington during his presidency was nothing more than a puppet of the French government would alter the meaning of the proper name. The name of an author is like any other proper name in oscillating "between the poles of description and designation," but "the link between a proper name and the individual being named and the link between an author's name and that which it names are not isomorphous and do not function in the same way" (122).

Foucault gives several examples, but one is sufficient to make his point. To say that Pierre Dupont does not exist is not the same as saying that Homer never existed. The first says only that there is no one whose name is Pierre Dupont, while the second says that "several individuals have been referred to by one name or that the real author possessed none of the traits traditionally associated with Homer" (122). Failure to recognize this difference between an author's name and other proper names can have disastrous results even outside of literary criticism: One might, for instance, point to Keith Donnellan's "Speaking of Nothing." Donnellan is trying in that paper to defend a theory of reference by explaining with his theory how apparent reference to the nonexistent is possible. In the course of the paper he uses as an example "*The Horn Papers,* [which] purported to contain the diary of one Jacob Horn" (1977, 210), and which, though some believers have thought them genuine, apparently are not. Donnellan claims that a person uttering the statement "Jacob Horn did not exist" would fail in his use of the expression "Jacob Horn" to refer to anything, without considering the possibility of that statement's referring to the author of *The Horn Papers* and asserting that his real name was not Jacob Horn. Later in the essay, Donnellan makes the same mistake in regard to the statement "Homer did not exist." Foucault, however, recognizes the presence of differences between an author's name and other proper names, and concludes that "an author's name is not simply an element of speech," but "its presence is functional in that it serves as a means of classification" (123). It groups texts together, differentiates them from others, and indicates certain relationships among them. It also "characterizes a particular manner of existence of discourse," granting to the discourse that possesses it a reception warmer than "the momentary attention given to ordinary, fleeting words" (123).

Foucault concludes that, while other proper names move "from the interior of a discourse to the real person outside," the name of the author is unique, and "remains at the contours of texts—separating one from the other, defining their form, and characterizing their mode of existence" (123). The name of the author in our culture

is a variable that accompanies only certain texts to the exclusion of others: a private letter may have a signatory, but it does not have an author: a contract can have an underwriter, but not an author; and, similarly, an anonymous poster attached to a wall may have a writer, but he cannot be an author. In this sense, the function of an author is to characterize the existence, circulation, and operation of certain discourses within a society. (124)

It is important that status as an author depends for Foucault on the *discourse* in question and not the *person*. Thus Wallace Stevens on Foucault's view is the author of the poem "The Curtains in the House of the Metaphysician," but even had he penned certain contracts for the Hartford Insurance Company he would not be the author of those contracts; similarly, *Deliverance* has an author, but not the advertising slogans James Dickey wrote for Coca-Cola during his tenure in that company's employ.

Having decided that the author is a function of discourse and that only some discourses have authors, Foucault next tries to isolate the features that distinguish texts with authors from those without. He isolates four such features. First, texts with authors are "objects of appropriation," a particular type of property. In our culture, Foucault says, speeches and books became this type of property (i.e., were assigned "real" authors other than "mythical or important religious figures") only when the author became subject to punishment. Second, "the 'author-function' is not universal or constant in all discourse" (125); whether a given type of text is assigned an author is not necessarily transhistorical or transcultural. In fact, our culture provides an example of a change in what types of discourse are assigned an author. What we now call "literary" texts were once "accepted, circulated, and valorized without any question about the identity of their author" (125), guaranteed of authenticity by their age alone. Texts that we now call "scientific," on the other hand, "were only considered truthful in the Middle Ages if the name of the author was indicated" as the mark of a "proven discourse" (125–26). In the seventeenth and eighteenth centuries, though, the roles were reversed so that literary texts required an author's name and scientific works came to be accepted on their own merits.[1]

Third, the "author-function" is not a spontaneous product of the simple attribution of a text to an individual.

> It results from a complex operation whose purpose is to construct the rational entity we call an author. . . . These aspects of an individual, which we designate as an author (or which comprise an individual as an author), are projections, in terms always more or less psychological, of our ways of handling texts. . . . In addition, [although there are some "transhistorical constants"] all these operations vary according to the period and the form of discourse concerned. A "philosopher" and a "poet" are not constructed in the same manner. (127).

In literary criticism, those operations are largely derived, Foucault says, from the operations "used in the Christian tradition to authenticate (or to reject) the particular texts in its possession." The fourth feature Foucault cites is that the "author-function" is not "a pure and simple reconstruction after the fact of a text given as passive material, since a text always bears a number of signs that refer to the author" (129). The author is not to be sought in the actual writer or in the fictional narrator; instead, "the 'author-function' arises out of their scission—in the division and distance of the two."

Next, Foucault points out that, while he has intentionally avoided speaking of the "author-function" in painting, music, and so on, his use of the term "author" has been too narrow even for the realm of discourse alone. He has spoken of the author only as "a person to whom the production of a text, a book, or a work can be legitimately attributed" (131). But,

Foucault claims, "even within the realm of discourse a person can be the author of much more than a book—of a theory, for instance, of a tradition or a discipline" (131). These authors occupy what Foucault calls a "transdiscursive" position, and Homer, Aristotle, and the Church Fathers are examples.

But there is in addition a special type of author, produced in nineteenth-century Europe; Foucault calls these authors "initiators of discursive practices." The two members of this class are Freud and Marx. "The distinctive contribution of these authors is that they produced not only their own work, but the possibility and the rules of formation of other texts" (131). Neither was merely the author of a few texts; instead, "they both established the endless possibility of discourse." This is different from what an important novelist does (Foucault's example is Ann Radcliffe and the Gothic Romance) because the "initiators of discursive practices" not only "made possible a certain number of analogies that could be adopted by future texts" (132), as an important novelist might do, but they also "made possible a certain number of differences," so that new elements may be added to the discourse other than their own while still remaining "within the field of discourse they initiated."

The initiation of discursive practices is also different from the founding of a new scientific endeavor (by Galileo or Newton, for example). The difference is that the founding act of a scientific endeavor "is on an equal footing with its future transformations: it is merely one among the many modifications that it makes possible" (133). The initiation of a discursive practice, however, "overshadows and is necessarily detached from its later developments and transformations" (134).

As a consequence, we define the theoretical validity of a statement [in a discursive practice] with respect to the

work of the initiator, whereas in the case of Galileo or
Newton, it is based on the structural and intrinsic norms
established in cosmology or physics. . . . A study of
Galileo's works could alter our knowledge of the history,
but not the science, of mechanics; whereas, a
reexamination of the books of Freud or Marx can
transform our understanding of psychoanalysis or
Marxism. (134–36)

Foucault takes the initiation of discursive practices as evidence
that the "author-function" has certain determining factors at
the level of a work or a series of works with a single signature,
but that it has additional determining factors at higher levels
like an entire discipline.

Foucault's final conclusion is formulated as a call for the
continuation of the project begun in "What Is an Author?" Such
a continuation could make possible, he says, a typology of
discourse, a historical analysis of discourse, and, most significant, a reexamination of the privileges of the subject. While the
subject "should not be entirely abandoned" (137), new questions should be asked about it:

Under what conditions and through what forms can an
entity like the subject appear in the order of discourse;
what position does it occupy; what functions does it
exhibit; and what rules does it follow in each type of discourse? In short, the subject must be stripped of its
creative role and analysed as a complex and variable
function of discourse. (137–38)

The author is one of "the possible specifications of the subject,"
and as such is subject to reevaluation. Foucault ends his essay
by imagining a culture where "discourse would circulate with-

out any need for an author . . . , [unfolding] in a pervasive anonymity" (138). In such a culture, the new questions asked about
the author would embody the claim implicit in the rhetorical
question with which the essay began and with which it ends:
"What matter who's speaking?"

Nehamas argues that the ideal of a culture with such indifference about the authorship of its discourses is not only a mistaken ideal, but an impossible one. He asserts instead that all
readings, even those of the sort at which Foucault aims, must
necessarily ask the question "Who *can be* speaking?" and that
the author is whatever answers that question (1987, 288). Nehamas isolates Foucault's assertion that, although all texts have
writers, not all have authors. He wants to "press the distinction
between writer and author" more consistently than does Foucault himself (1987, 272). Nehamas makes the distinction in
this way:

> Writers are actual individuals, firmly located in history,
> efficient causes of their texts. They often misunderstand
> their own work and are as confused about it as we
> frequently are about the sense and significance, indeed the
> very nature, of our actions. Writers truly exist outside
> their texts. They have no interpretive authority over them.
>
> An author, by contrast, is whoever can be understood to
> have produced a particular text as we interpret it. Authors
> are not individuals but characters manifested or
> exemplified, though not depicted or described, in texts.
> They are formal causes. They are postulated to account for
> a text's features and are produced through an interaction
> between critic and text. Their nature guides interpretation,
> and interpretation determines their nature.(1986, 686)

According to "Writer, Text, Work, Author," what happens is
this: "Writers produce texts. Some texts are subject to interpre-

tation: Understanding them involves seeing them as the products of idiosyncratic agents. Interpretation construes texts as works. Works generate the figure of the author" (1987, 281). The author (1) "is a plausible historical variant of the writer," (2) is "the joint product of writer and text, of critic and interpretation," and (3) is "everything the work shows it to be and . . . [it] can in turn determine what the text shows" (285). The author, then, functions as a limiting force insuring an "accurate" interpretation: "What a text means is what it could mean to its writer" (1981, 149), and a text's author is what the text indicates the writer could have been.

There are several questions to ask about Nehamas's view. First, if writers can be mistaken about the meaning of their texts, why privilege what the writer could have meant as the meaning of a text? Second, what kind of constraints does an answer to the question "Who *can be* speaking?" put on the meaning of a text, and do those constraints insure an "accurate" reading of the sort Nehamas wants? And third, is there any reason to believe two of Nehamas's most important assumptions: (1) that although texts are inexhaustible, they are not manifold, and (2) that given two competing interpretations, one is always better than the other?

Nehamas is very clear in his insistence that the writer of a text can be mistaken about its meaning. I have already quoted a passage in which Nehamas makes a writer's misunderstanding of and confusion about his own work one of the characteristics that distinguishes a writer from an author. The point is also made, though, in other ways and in other places within Nehamas's essays. For instance, he asserts in "The Postulated Author" that "meaning . . . depends on an author's intentions even if a writer is not aware of it" (1981, 145). But Nehamas is equally insistent that the author's intentions are determined by what the writer's intentions could have been, so that the sentence immediately following the one just quoted says that "the author's intentions depend on what the writer could have meant." Or again: "The author . . . [is] a character the writer could have been, someone who means what the writer could have meant" (1987, 285).

The notion that a writer can be mistaken about what she means is of course not new to Nehamas or to the structuralist and deconstructive criticism to which he is opposed, or for that matter even to the New Critics, who were the first to make that notion a central tenet in their critical theory. Hegel, for example, almost two centuries ago wrote in the *Phenomenology:* "We learn by experience that we meant something other than we meant to mean" (1977, 39).[2] But if a text need not mean what its writer actually meant it to mean, then why must it mean what she could have meant it to mean? If, as Nehamas admits, the aim of interpretation is not to "re-create or replicate a state of mind which someone else has already undergone" (1987, 285), then why demand that interpretation abide by the limits of what such a state of mind could have been? Nehamas's answer is this: Freeing the text from what the writer could have meant would necessitate an extreme revisionism (1987, 284ff.), which would be unsatisfactory presumably because it would result in some sort of interpretive meltdown, provoked by the removal of historical constraints, in which every reading would affect several others until all of literature burned out of control.

This answer is given in the form of a response to Borges's suggestion that we attribute the *Imitatio Christi* to Céline or Joyce. Nehamas responds that we could, "but James Joyce is, among many other things, the Irish Catholic author of *Ulysses*" (1987, 284). Unfortunately, such a response is inadequate precisely because it does not meet Nehamas's goal of pressing consistently the distinction between author and writer. Only the writer, not the author, as Nehamas defines them, gives any a priori reason to "have to read it as the work of the Irish Catholic author of *Ulysses*." The Joyce to whom Nehamas refers here as the *author* of *Ulysses* is, to be consistent with Nehamas's own terminology, not the author but the *writer* of *Ulysses*; and the consequence, more accurately stated, is that we would have to read the work written by the late medieval German monk as if it had been written by the modern Irish writer of *Ulysses*. But there is no reason to assume with Nehamas that such a reading obligates the reader permanently or that it necessarily has such extensive ramifications. If a scientist wished to test the behavior of a certain chemical at very low temperature and pressure, no one would consider her obligated to test every chemical under such conditions, nor would anyone assume that all chemicals would behave in the same way under the same conditions or that that chemical would act in the same way under all conditions.

It is true enough that historical connection with a given writer is typically the most important indicator of which works are best read as an oeuvre (which will most easily or most satisfactorily produce a coherent figure of the sort I will later call the synoptic proxy), and surely no one, not even Foucault or Derrida, would argue against this as a useful general principle, any more than they would violate it in practice without some reason. However, as I will show later in this book (and I take it Foucault is arguing, at least indirectly, for a similar point), there *are* reasons to violate this general principle. Furthermore, it is easy to imagine cases in which the author has with the writer no historical connection of the sort Nehamas assumes, in which the author's intentions, in other words, do *not* "depend on what the writer could have meant" (1981, 145). Imagine a thoughtful, devoted husband who on a whim types the words "I love you" on a small sheet of paper and leaves the paper on his wife's pillow for her to find. When he finds the same sheet of paper on his own pillow the following night, the meaning of the text—that his wife loves him—will be clear enough, but the author (the wife) will not be a "historically plausible variant" of the writer (the husband), nor will the wife's intentions "depend on what the [husband] could have meant," since by the words "I love you" he could only have meant that he loves her and not that she loves him. This same illustration might also serve as a counterexample to another of Nehamas's assumptions, one that is central to his project of defending critical monism, namely, that a text can fulfill only one set of intentions. The love note is clearly able to fulfill the intentions of the wife as well as those of the husband; and it is fair to assume that it would also serve the intentions of one of the husband's bowling buddies if he borrowed the note to leave on *his* wife's pillow, or even the intentions of the wife's secret lover, which stand in direct conflict with the intentions of the faithful husband.

One might defend Nehamas by suggesting that the love note is a text that is understood without really being interpreted, appealing to his claim that we can understand texts "without necessarily interpreting them" (1987, 275). He fills out the meaning of this claim by saying that, although understanding always involves interpretation, there are cases in which understanding is based only on "obvious, generally shared, and uncontroversial conventions or background assumptions" (275) and that in such cases "interpretation can be so automatic that it constitutes a limiting, null case" (276). It is only when "special assumptions" or "idiosyncratic hypotheses" are involved that "genuine" or "literary" interpretation becomes necessary, and it is only in cases of "genuine" or "literary" interpretation that the text is authored. However, Nehamas distinguishes between the two possibilities by this criterion: "In interpretation strictly conceived we account for the features of an object by appealing to the features of an unusual, original agent whose action we take it to be and who is manifested in it. We take the action, by means of an explicit and often complex process, as an unusual, original event—an event characteristic of its agent, to be sure, but not of many (or any) others" (277). The reader of the love note does seem forced, if he or she is to understand the note, to appeal to the features of an unusual, original agent, namely, his or her spouse, and to construe it as an event characteristic of only that one agent and no others. It appears, therefore, to be a case of "genuine" interpretation on Nehamas's view, and to be a text with an author; but it undercuts others of Nehamas's assumptions because the author's historical connections are with the sender, and not necessarily the writer, of the text.

The same assumptions could be challenged on the basis of an "actual" example instead of an imagined one. By Nehamas's criterion just quoted, a birthday card on the shelf at the Hallmark store would be an example of a text without an author, a text not susceptible to a "genuine" interpretation. No unusual, original agent is manifested in it. However, the same birthday card signed by someone and given to another *is* a text with an author, whose features are accounted for by appealing to the features of an unusual, original agent who is manifested in it. But the agent is historically connected not with the writer of the card, but with the person who selected, signed, and sent it.

The second question I want to ask about Nehamas's view is what sort of constraints an answer to the question "Who *can be* speaking?" puts on the meaning of a text, and whether those constraints insure an "accurate" reading of the sort Nehamas wants. Nehamas's first mention of Foucault in "The Postulated Author" is as a member of a paragraph-long list of misguided "deconstructive critics," and his summary of Foucault's view there is a curious one: "Foucault. . . claims that the author is a fiction created, more or less, by St. Jerome, now moribund and an object of indifference" (1981, 136). The summary is curious because St. Jerome appears in Foucault's essay only as an example to support the third of four features of the "author-function" listed in the middle of the essay, not as the sole creator of the author in the Western tradition. The feature is that the author is a projection "of our way of handling texts" (Foucault 1977, 127), and Foucault says that the methods for "determining the configuration of the author from existing texts" in literary criticism "derive in large part from those used in the Christian tradition to authenticate (or to reject) the particular texts in its possession" (127). St. Jerome is one node in that Christian tradition, and he gives four criteria for eliminating a text from a list of works attributed to a single author. Foucault describes those four criteria in this way:

> The texts that must be eliminated . . . are those inferior to the others (thus, the author is defined as a standard level of quality); those whose ideas conflict with the doctrine expressed in the others (here the author is defined as a certain field of conceptual or theoretical coherence); those written in a different style and containing words and phrases not ordinarily found in the other works (the author is seen as a stylistic uniformity); and those referring to events or historical figures subsequent to the death of the author (the author is thus a definite historical figure in which a series of events converge). (128)

Nehamas is attempting to revive the use of at least the fourth of St. Jerome's principles, but he takes its worth as an assumption, without defending it. A defense is called for, however, since Foucault has argued that St. Jerome's four criteria serve the purpose of establishing the *canonicity* of a text, while Nehamas is concerned about the *meaning* of a text. Nehamas claims that "to interpret a text is to consider it as its author's production" (1981, 145), *not* as its writer's production. And while (as I shall argue below) this is what is needed in order to link meaning and historical plausibility, it is not consistent with Nehamas's other statements. The reason is that here again Nehamas fails to achieve his goal of pressing consistently the distinction between writer and author, for he claims that (1) "literary texts are produced by agents and must be understood as such," and (2) "since texts are products of expressive actions, understanding them is inseparably tied to understanding their agents" (1981, 145). On those two assumptions, the agent to be understood must be the writer, since she is the only one who actually produced the text.

But an author of a text is distinct from its writer, and a text is understood by understanding the author, so the agent who produces the text is not the same agent who is understood in order to understand the text. If the author "is postulated as the agent whose actions account for the text's features," then given that he is distinct from the writer, the restriction of the postulated agent to the limitations of the historical agent seems, in the absence of a defense, arbitrary. Nehamas does not explain why it is that if an explanatory agent outside the limitations of the historical agent can be postulated who can better account for the text's features than can an agent within those limitations, the former is not to be preferred over the latter; nor does he explicitly claim that it is impossible to produce an explanatory agent outside the limitations of the historical agent who can better account for the text's features than can an agent within those limitations.

Common sense, long tradition, and current practice (even structuralist/deconstructive practice) all recommend the maintenance of some kind of connection between writer and author, but to spell out what that connection is would require more consistency in pressing the distinction between writer and author than Nehamas musters. Nehamas blurs the distinction by his use of the phrase "account for the text's features" (1981, 145). It is one thing to account for (explain) the *presence* of a given feature of a text. The writer is able to account for a feature in that sense. But it is quite another thing to account for (interpret) the *meaning* of a given feature of a text. This is what the author is to do. But Nehamas has already stated specifically that the writer does not (and need not be able to) account for the meaning of the features of a text, and he has directly implied that no author is needed to account for the presence of a text's features (since texts do not always have authors, but their features can always be accounted for), so it is not clear on his view how it is that the writer puts constraints on the author.

The important difference between accounting for the presence of a text's features and accounting for the meaning of those features is illustrated by the old puzzle of probability concerning the length of time it would take for a thousand monkeys at a thousand typewriters to produce an encyclopedia. It is surely possible, though obviously unlikely, that a thousand monkeys at a thousand typewriters could by sheer chance produce an encyclopedia. If they did, they would be able to account for the presence of all the features of the text: Everything in the text was put there, quite fortuitously, by monkeys at Smith-Coronas. But on Nehamas's view, there would be no way to account for the meaning of the text's features, because, since the monkeys could not have meant anything by their typing, there is no way to produce an author who can mean anything the writer could have meant.

In order to resolve this dilemma, to provide a *justification* for allowing historical plausibility to limit interpretation, it is necessary to begin with exactly the tenet that Nehamas most vigorously opposes. He says that "deconstructive critics begin with the realization that written texts are enormously independent of their writers and then proceed to sever altogether, at least in theory, the connection between author and text" (1981, 135). What he must mean is that deconstructive critics sever the connection between *writer* and text, since by his own definitions it would be impossible in any case of "genuine" interpretation to sever the connection between author and text. But the claim that Nehamas most despises (that a text is severed from its writer) is precisely the claim that is needed in order to make possible the consequence he most desires (to provide a justification for the meaning of a text to be linked to "historical plausibility").

As long as the writer is thought of as being attached to the text, it is she who accounts for the presence of the text's features. And as I have argued above, when the writer is used to account for the presence of the text's features and the author to account for their meaning, there is no justification for imposing the writer's limitations on the author. However, once it is acknowledged that after the creative act is complete writer and text are independent, then (as I will show later) the author must account for both the presence and the meaning of the text's features. The fact that a single agent[3] must account for presence *and* meaning justifies (indeed requires) that there be a connection between the two. When instead of holding the writer accountable for the presence of the text's features and the author accountable for their meaning, the author is held responsible for both the presence and the meaning of the text's features, then there is justification for requiring the two accounts to be compatible.

It is easy to see why someone arguing for critical monism would be anxious to retain a "historical plausibility" requirement. But Nehamas does not succeed in making historical plausibility serve the interests of monism. In order to insure a text's having a single meaning (and therefore only one "accurate" reading), the writer would have to account for the meaning as well as the presence of the text's features. But Nehamas admits that that is impossible. The only way to retain a justifiable "historical plausibility" requirement is to require the author to account for the presence and the meaning of the text's features; but the author, who is at the mercy of text and reader, is not capable of insuring monism.

The third question I want to ask is whether there is any reason to believe two of Nehamas's most important assumptions: (1) that although texts are inexhaustible, they are not manifold, and (2) that given two competing interpretations, one is always better than the other. Both of these assumptions are essential to Nehamas's attempt (from which his discussion of the author arises and the ends of which his discussion of the author serves) to defend "critical monism as a regulative ideal." Both assumptions are linked to the analogy of criticism and science with which "The Postulated Author" begins:

> Critical pluralism, broadly stated, is the view that literary texts, unlike natural phenomena, for which there is only one correct explanation, can be given many equally acceptable, even though incompatible, interpretations. But the thesis that, in contrast to science, "the use . . . of diverse but complementary vantages [is] not only rationally justifiable, but necessary to the understanding of art, and indeed of any subject of humanistic inquiry" [the words of M. H. Abrams] seems to me to make a virtue out of necessity and a necessity out of fact. (1981, 133)

The fact to which he refers is that literary works *do* result in a variety of interpretations.

The important question here is whether the analogy of criticism with science, a common enough analogy, is a good one. The answer is that it is not. It assumes two further analogies, neither of which is satisfactory. First, it assumes that works of art are precisely analogous to natural phenomena. But the human origin of the former in contrast to the nonhuman origin of the latter is enough of a disanalogy to undermine that assumption. A work of art manipulates natural phenomena, and makes them *un*natural at least in the sense of making them artificial. Second, the analogy of criticism with science assumes that interpretation is precisely analogous to explanation. But scientific explanation is concerned primarily with describing something or accounting (typically in terms of causation) for its origin, while interpretation is concerned primarily with discovering the significance or meaning of the thing.[4] Thus, when a scientist speaks of the mutation of a virus and its spread through the transfer of blood or semen, she is offering an *explanation* of AIDS; but when the president of the Southern Baptist Convention speaks of the AIDS epidemic as God's judgment on homosexuals, he is offering an *interpretation* of the same phenomenon.

It may be true that, given two competing explanations of a natural phenomenon, one must be better than the other (however one wishes to fill out the meaning of "better"). But even if this is true (an issue it is not necessary to decide here), it still does not follow that, given two competing interpretations of a work of art, one must be better than the other. Even if Newton's laws and quantum theory are mutually exclusive theories of mechanics, that is no reason in itself to conclude that Frost's "Stopping by Woods on a Snowy Evening" is not about the beauty of nature *and* about suicide. Yet Nehamas arrives at just such a conclusion on the basis of the scientific analogy. He uses as his illustration Stanley Corngold's *The Commentator's*

Despair: The Interpretation of Kafka's "Metamorphosis," whose thesis Nehamas summarizes in this way: "Corngold interprets Samsa's change into what is an essentially vague, incomplete, and indescribable monster as an allegory for writing itself—an activity which, according to many recent literary theorists [among whose number, one supposes, Nehamas includes Foucault], is bound to result in imperfect communication, unavoidable misunderstanding, and inevitable misreading" (1981, 134).

Nehamas argues, against this thesis, that

> Corngold's view is reached through an interpretation
> which must be itself correct if it is to explain why there
> cannot be a correct interpretation of the story. And this
> paradox of method is parallel to a paradox of content. *The
> Metamorphosis,* on this view, concerns the inability of
> literature to achieve perfect communication and so to
> receive final interpretation. This is what the story communi-
> cates. (134)

Both paradoxes of which Nehamas accuses Corngold—that of method and that of content—are paradoxes only if one grants Nehamas his twin assumptions that no text can support a multiplicity of meanings and that, given two differing interpretations, one will always be better than the other. I argue, though, that neither assumption is correct, and that Nehamas has here posed a false dilemma. He claims that either the creature's being an allegory for writing itself is the single correct interpretation of the work, in which case the story communicates perfectly that literature cannot communicate perfectly, or else the creature cannot be an allegory for writing at all. But if one denies his assumptions, a third possibility emerges: that Kafka's *Metamorphosis,* whether or not it communicates anything at all, is able to support the interpretation of the creature as an allegory for writing itself, where writing is conceived of as something other than perfect communication. Without the burden of Nehamas's assumptions, the fact that *The Metamorphosis* is able to support that interpretation would neither deny the story's ability to support other interpretations, nor would it render that interpretation paradoxical.

So it is that one need not always make a necessity out of a fact; and from the fact of multiple divergent readings of literary works one might just as easily make, instead of a necessity, a possibility. There is no reason to believe with Nehamas that without supposing there to be for any given text a uniquely correct interpretation toward which the act of interpretation aims and which manifests itself in direct proportion to the accuracy of the scale-model author the reader pastes together, complete critical anarchy will inevitably follow. Nor is there any reason to suppose with Foucault that interpretation *ought* to endorse the already radical separation of a text from its writer, indeed ought to make that separation, at least for the purposes of interpretation, absolute. For in spite of the complexity and fecundity of his essay, Foucault is guilty of the charge Nehamas levels against him (and the one that I have leveled in turn against Nehamas), namely, not pressing consistently the distinction between author and writer. The questions Foucault wants to excommunicate from the kingdom of criticism ("Who is the real author?," "Have we proof of his authenticity and originality?," and "What has he revealed of his most profound self in his language?") all ask about the writer, indicating that what Foucault thinks ought to be indifferent is not who *is speaking* but who *has spoken.* Yet the distinction between writer and author, and the separation of the writer from his text, need not imply that the reader should be indifferent to who has spoken, any more than the writer's being the origin of a work means that he can or should control its meaning.

I have argued that Nehamas is mistaken when he claims that "who could have spoken" is the determinant of the uniquely correct meaning of a text. And I have suggested that Foucault's claim that "who has spoken" is utterly irrelevant is equally bad. Neither Foucault nor Nehamas, I contend, has provided an account of the author that is able to support his view, and neither has provided an account sufficiently accurate or useful to tell us "what an author is." For this reason it has seemed more profitable, maintaining the distinction between writer and author (or, as I will later call them, the creative author and the created author) and acknowledging the importance of each, to investigate the creative author with an eye toward understanding how the work's history shapes and delimits its possibilities, as well as the ways in which the creative author can or should influence the reader's conception of the created author, and to investigate the created author with an eye toward understanding how she is conceived in the intercourse between reader and text and how her presence influences interpretation.

CHAPTER 3

Barthes and Gass

I said at the beginning of the previous chapter that Foucault and Nehamas are concerned with *how* to recognize an author, and that Barthes and Gass are concerned with *whether* to recognize an author. The result is that Foucault and Nehamas focus on the boundary between the author and the writer. To decide what an author is requires a determination of whether and how an author differs from a writer. Foucault and Nehamas ask a question of identity. Barthes and Gass, on the other hand, focus on the boundary between the author and the reader. Their question, whether to acknowledge the author, requires a determination of whether it is the author or the reader who has enough power to decide how much influence over interpretation the other will be granted. Barthes and Gass ask a question of power.

Barthes begins by asking about a brief quotation from Balzac's *Sarrasine* just the question Foucault hoped to eliminate: "Who is speaking thus?" The apparent disagreement between Barthes and Foucault is resolved, though, by the end of the first paragraph, when Barthes gives the assumption about writing from which his conclusions about authorship will follow:

> We shall never know [who is speaking thus], for the good
> reason that writing is the destruction of every voice, of

every point of origin. Writing is that neutral, composite, oblique space where our subject slips away, the negative where all identity is lost, starting with the very identity of the body writing. (1977, 142)

Just as Foucault's "What matter who's speaking?" has to mean "What matter who has spoken?," so Barthes's "Who is speaking thus?" must mean "Who has spoken thus?" Barthes gives himself away by indications such as the equivalence of "voice" and "point of origin." It is initially and primarily the "body writing" whose voice is lost. Thus Foucault's attempt to eliminate the question of who is speaking and Barthes's answer to that very question actually assert much the same thing: that the writing subject is not preserved in that which is written, and therefore is not and should not be a determining factor in interpretation.

Barthes is rebelling against a model of reading that could be compared to the Presocratics' search for the arché. Aristotle says the earliest philosophers sought a single material principle, "that of which all things that are consist, the first from which they came to be, the last into which they are resolved." This principle is the source of all things and is always conserved (1941b, A 3, 983b). Thus, the first step toward understanding the world is to locate this principle. Criticism has often taken the author to be similar to the arché not only in the sense of being the source of the work, but also as being conserved in it. Barthes, though, makes it clear in the passage quoted above that at least one of the things he means by the death of the author is that the writer, the text's arché, is not conserved in the text.

Barthes says that, although writing has always been "the negative where all identity is lost," our sense of "this disconnection" has varied. "In ethnographic societies the responsibility for a narrative is never assumed by a person but by a mediator, shaman or relator whose 'performance'—the mastery of the narrative code—may possibly be admired but never his 'genius' " (142). "The author," he says (in agreement with Foucault), "is a modern figure" produced by our society's discovery, when "English empiricism, French rationalism, and the personal faith of the Reformation" emerged from the Middle Ages, of "the prestige of the individual, of, as it is more nobly put, the 'human person' " (143). The author's "reign" in anthologies, biographies of writers, interviews, and so on, is thus for Barthes a "positivism, the epitome and culmination of capitalist ideology." That is why the importance commonly attached to the author's "person" is for Barthes a problem to be solved:

> The image of literature to be found in ordinary culture is tyrannically centered on the author, his person, his life, his tastes, his passions. . . . The *explanation* of a work is always sought in the man or woman who produced it, as if it were always in the end, through the more or less transparent allegory of the fiction, the voice of a single person, the *author* 'confiding' in us. (143)

The attempt to dethrone the author, though, is hardly new with Barthes. It is easy to find examples of this project in many earlier twentieth-century critics. For instance, T. S. Eliot wrote in "Tradition and the Individual Talent" that "the progress of an artist is a continual self-sacrifice, a continual extinction of personality" (1975, 40). To the New Critics, the "intentional fallacy" was a mortal sin. And Northrop Frye says in *Anatomy of Criticism:*

> The absurd quantum formula of criticism, the assertion that the critic should confine himself to "getting out" of a poem exactly what the poet may vaguely be assumed to

43

have been aware of "putting in," is one of the many
slovenly illiteracies that the absence of systematic
criticism has allowed to grow up. This quantum theory is
the literary form of what may be called the fallacy of
premature teleology. (1957, 17)

How, then, is Barthes's proclamation of the *death* of the author
any different from the *dethronement* of the author proclaimed
by such statements as these? Gregory T. Polletta points out
one way in which Barthes is different: Most critics expelled
authorial intention "in order to ensure the correct interpretation of literary works. Barthes, on the other hand, excludes the
author's declared intention in order to release the text from any
authoritarian control or interpretative circumscription" (1984,
111).[1]

Barthes takes Mallarmé to be his predecessor in this "releasing" of the text from the author. The release takes a particular
shape: It comes as a substitution of "language itself for the
person who until [Mallarmé] had been supposed to be its owner"
(143). For Mallarmé and subsequently for Barthes, "it is language itself which speaks, not the author; to write is . . . to
reach that point where only language acts, 'performs', and not
'me'." Valéry was next after Mallarmé: "He never stopped calling into question and deriding the Author" (144). Proust followed suit by "inexorably blurring . . . the relation between the
writer and his characters," making "of his very life a work for
which his own book was the model." And finally, Surrealism
"contributed to the desacrilization of the image of the Author"
by disappointing expectations of meaning, by automatic writing, and by "accepting the principle and experience of several
people writing together." Barthes also claims that, in addition
to these elements of the French literary tradition, linguistics

has aided "the destruction of the Author" (145). It does so, Barthes says,

> by showing that the whole of enunciation is an empty process, functioning perfectly without there being any need for it to be filled with the person of the interlocutors. Linguistically, the author is never more than the instance writing . . .: language knows a 'subject', not a 'person', and this subject, empty outside of the very enunciation which defines it, suffices to make language 'hold together', suffices, that is to say, to exhaust it. (145)

The word "writing" appears in Barthes's essay with two different meanings: (1) the act of writing, and (2) that which is written. So far in his essay, Barthes has concentrated almost exclusively on the first sense of the word, as if what he means by "author" is what Nehamas called the writer. But here the focus shifts. That language functions without any need for the person of the interlocutors changes, according to Barthes, the temporality of the text. The author is no longer "the past of his own book," standing in relation to it as father to child, nourishing it. Instead, "the modern scriptor is born simultaneously with the text, is in no way equipped with a being preceding or exceeding the writing, is not the subject with the book as predicate": The text is no longer written by an author once and for all, but "every text is eternally written *here and now*." This means that Barthes is free to conflate writing (act) and writing (what is written); there is no longer any difference. "Writing" is no longer "an operation of recording, notation, representation, 'depiction'," but is "what linguists . . . call a performative . . . in which the enunciation has no other content . . . than the act by which it is uttered—something like the *I declare* of kings or the *I sing* of very ancient poets" (145–46).

More important, though, for Barthes, the change in temporality means that only writings can write, not authors. The text has changed from "a line of words releasing a single, 'theological' meaning" into "a multi-dimensional space in which a variety of writings, none of them original, blend and clash." The writer cannot express himself because the state or "inner 'thing' " he tries to "translate" into words "is itself only a ready-formed dictionary, its words only explainable through other words, and so on indefinitely." The writer can do no more than to mix writings that are themselves not original, so that he "no longer bears within him passions, humours, feelings, impressions, but rather this immense dictionary from which he draws a writing that can know no halt: life never does more than imitate the book, and the book itself is only a tissue of signs, an imitation that is lost, infinitely deferred" (147). The transition is complete: The word "writing" has been changed from designating an activity to supplanting the word "literature."

Now Gregory Polletta's statement, quoted above, explaining how Barthes's "death of the author" differs from other attempts to dethrone the author, is clearer. Barthes releases the text "from any authoritarian control" by releasing it from the hands of the "Author-God" into the hands of the reader, and he relegates the author to the rank of "scriptor." Giving a text an Author-God imposes a limit on it, but the imposition, Barthes says, is unwarranted, since the text has no limits:

> In the multiplicity of writing, everything is to be *disentangled*, nothing *deciphered*; the structure can be followed, 'run' (like the thread of a stocking) at every point and at every level, but there is nothing beneath: the space of writing is to be ranged over, not pierced; writing ceaselessly posits meaning ceaselessly to evaporate it, carrying out a systematic exemption of meaning. (147)

Previously, the text was a cloth to be unraveled by the reader; if the cloth were unwound all the way, the reader would find the author holding the other end. But Barthes makes the text into a shroud, and no one, not even a corpse, is holding the other end.

Barthes argues for a sort of "textual anarchy." His essay is a demand for, and a proclamation of, revolution: Power over the text should belong not to the author but to each individual reader. Any given writing is only a concatenation of numerous other writings, and these writings are focused not in the person of the author but in the reader. Though the reader is no more a person than the author (he is "without history, biography, psychology"), yet he is "the space on which all the quotations that make up a writing are inscribed without any of them being lost" (148). The reader must assert his power over the text because "a text's unity lies not in its origin but in its destination." The past has belonged to "Classic criticism" and to the author, that despot criticism put into office, but in order to give the future to writing, "it is necessary to overthrow the myth: the birth of the reader must be at the cost of the death of the Author" (148).

William Gass, however, rejects Barthes's conclusion, arguing not for a "textual anarchy" but for a benevolent dictatorship in which the author unselfishly rules her text. Gass begins by pointing out a disanalogy between the death of the author and the death of God: He says that everyone (including Barthes and "the current members of this faith") knows that there *are* authors and that there *are no* gods. This makes the two expressions not only disanalogous but "the reverse of one another":

The death of god represents not only the realization that gods have never existed, but the contention that such a belief is no longer even irrationally possible. . . . The belief lingers on, of course, but it does so like astrology or a faith in a flat earth. . . . The death of the author, on the other hand, signifies a decline in authority, in theological power, as if Zeus were stripped of his thunderbolts and swans, perhaps residing on Olympus still, but now living in a camper and cooking with propane. He *is*, but he is no longer a god. (1986a, 265)

Gass does acknowledge, though, at least one similarity between authors and gods: Both "are in the business of design." Then he argues, using quotations from Ransom and Joyce, that even when the author apparently withdraws from his work, even when he is "invisible" or "nearly anonymous," yet his disappearance "coincides with his arrogance, his overbearing presence" (266). The disappearance of the author is not enough for Barthes, Gass says, because it constitutes an increase instead of a decline in authority or theological power, so Barthes must long for "the demise of just that confident, coldly overbearing, creator—that so palpably erased and disdainfully imperial person of the artist" (267).

　If Barthes longs for the imperial artist's demise, Gass longs for that same imperial artist's eternal life. Barthes tries to shift the meaning of the term "writing" to include only what is written and to exclude the act of writing; Gass reverses this, and tries to shift the meaning to include only the act of writing and to exclude what is written. Gass says that, "when the work of writing has been done, the essential artistic task is over." The text on his view is "a thing whose modulated surfaces betray the consciousness it contains, and which we read, as we read words, to find the hand, the arm, the head, the voice, the self, which is shaping them, which is arranging those surfaces—

this second skin—to reflect an inside sun, and reveal the climate of an inner life" (267).

Barthes's essay, with its call for a revolution of sorts, has definite moral overtones. Gass's essay is no less morally weighted, and in fact the claim that written works contain a consciousness that it is the purpose of reading to discover sounds strikingly similar to Milton's vehement argument "For the Liberty of Unlicenc'd Printing" in *Areopagitica*. Arguing against a 1643 parliamentary ordinance for licensing of the press, which after a 1637 decree effectively gave Archbishop Laud control of every press in England (Hughes 1957, 716), Milton wrote:

> I deny not but that it is of greatest concernment in the church and commonwealth to have a vigilant eye how books demean themselves as well as men. . . . For books are not absolutely dead things, but do contain a potency of life in them to be as active as that soul was whose progeny they are; nay, they do preserve as in a vial the purest efficacy and extraction of that living intellect that bred them. . . . And yet . . . unless wariness be used, as good almost kill a man as kill a good book: who kills a man kills a reasonable creature, God's image; but he who destroys a good book, kills reason itself, kills the image of God, as it were, in the eye. Many a man lives a burden to the earth; but a good book is the precious lifeblood of a master spirit, embalmed and treasured up on purpose to a life beyond life. (Milton 1957, 720)

Milton's argument might be summarized in this way:

(1) A book is a living embodiment of its author's soul.
(2) To destroy (suppress publication or distribution of) a book is to kill it.

-----

(3) To destroy a book is analogous to (and as wrong as)
    killing a person.

Gass's argument depends on the same first premise; the terms
in the other premises are merely altered to direct the argument
away from the frontal assault made on books by Parliament's
denial of the author's right to publish freely what has been
created, and against what Gass sees as an attack from the rear
in the form of Barthes's denial of the author's power to create
what will be published (or to have created what has been published):

(1) A book is a living embodiment of its author's soul.
(2) To destroy (to refuse the authority of) the author is
    to kill him.

-----

(3) To kill a person (the author) is as wrong as (because
    it amounts to) killing his book.

Although Gass has implied already that Barthes must long not
merely for the disappearance but for the demise of the author,
he himself concentrates primarily on the author's (intentional)
disappearance, trying to show that "when the artist hides, it is
in order to represent skill as instinct, intellect as reflex, choice
as necessity, labor as slumberous ease" (267). The artist's deliberate disappearance should no more signify his death to the
reader than an armed criminal's disappearance into an abandoned warehouse should signify his death to a policeman, and
the reader should be no less on guard on his manhunt than the
policeman on his. Gass describes the pseudonyms used in books
like *Gulliver's Travels, Clarissa Harlowe,* and *The History of
Henry Esmond* as "dildos," and reminds his readers (if any
had forgotten) that although the "real" authors of these books

pretend that the "artificial" authors are responsible for writing them, yet the "real" authors intended to "accept all praises and monies due" (269).

Gass then runs through various possibilities that he opposes to the "fictional anonymity" of writers like Swift and Defoe. Trollope is "a comfortable theist who appears on page after page in order to sustain and continue and comfort his creation" (269). Gass assumes that the narrator who in Trollope's works "converses" with the reader is Trollope himself "appear[ing] . . . by our fireside," and this theism is different from the deism of writers like Flaubert, Henry James, and Joyce, "who wind their works up and then let them run as they may." Even pantheism is possible, and Gass takes Rilke's *Notebooks of Malte Laurids Brigge* as his example: The book is "so infused with the poet's presence, the poet's particular sensibilities, that Malte, his surrogate, cannot avoid surrendering his self to his author's *style*, even when the outcome of his life appears to be different from his creator's" (270).

There are also, says Gass, a number of other kinds of "authorless" works besides those in which the writer hides behind a pseudonym. There are, for example, parlor games "in which a poem is composed one line at a time by inebriated guests," novels produced by authors writing alternate chapters, and the "more serious" *renga* chain poem. But neither "authorless" works nor works "with a great degree of authorial visibility" are made any better or worse by the author's visibility alone. Instead, "it should be recognized that the elevation or removal of the author is a social and political and psychological gesture, and not an esthetic one" (273). Authorship may be denied or hidden for various reasons (for example, "to extol certain sources or origins" [270]), and "this 'anonymity'. . . may mean many things, but one thing which it cannot mean is that *no one did it.*"

The claim Gass has been leading up to is that the effacement of the author does not elevate the reader, as Barthes argues, but instead renders the reader helpless, "unnecessary." The highly visible Trollope "merely insert[s] his characters into the well-known world of his readers," but Flaubert, instead of merely telling a story, "is constructing a world; he is putting it together atom by atom, word by word." Flaubert "wishes to shape [the text] so securely a reader will not be necessary" (274). Thus, on Gass's view, the author's disappearance is not enough for Barthes, because the author's disappearance is not a sign of his death, but his means of deification; it is how "the author becomes a god." And, according to Gass, this contradicts Barthes's thesis. Instead of the author's absence constituting a transfer of power into the hands of the reader, Gass asserts that just the opposite occurs: "When the author detaches himself from the text, he detaches the reader at the same time" (274).

In other words, while the reader is decisively separated from the text when the author disappears, the author himself manages to remain in the text even when he departs. "If the author goes, taking the reader with him, into some justifiable oblivion, he does not omit to leave his signature behind, just the same" (275). Gass goes even further: He says that in fact whether the author remains in the work is not even a problem. The only question for Gass is "whether the text can take care of itself, can stand on its own, or whether it needs whatever outside help it can get" (276–77). He outlines "six regularly scheduled trains out of the text." They are:

(1) Literary Tradition/Influences
(2) Construction of the Text: How to Write
(3) Hermeneutical Heaven: Replacement of the Text with Its Interpretation
(4) Reader as Interpreting Subject or Rhetorical Object

(5) Historical Context/Bio of the Writer
(6) World as Referent/"Truth about Life"

Gass says that Barthes, in spite of his "appearing to free the text from such externals," ties the text "rather firmly" to two of the trains out of the text: "the literary tradition on the one hand, and the reader's caprices on the other" (279).

Gass is willing to concede to Barthes that there are innumerable authorless texts, among them office memos and presidential speeches, but he insists on the same distinction Nehamas makes: that a text is authored if we ask of it who is responsible, who wrote it. However, Gass's claim that the test of whether a text is or is not authored occurs after the creation of the text and is administered by the reader requires a further concession: He must admit that the writer and the author are not strictly identical.

> From the poem the reader projects the poet . . .—not a person but the poet of the poem. . . . The artificial author (the author which the text creates, not the author who creates the text) will be importantly different from the one of flesh and blood, envy and animosity, who holds the pen, and whose picture enlivens the gray pages of history. (282–83)

Furthermore, when an author devotes most of his life to one work (Gass's examples are Dante, Spenser, and Proust), the resulting works "not only imply an artificial author, they profoundly alter, sometimes, the nature of the historical one" (284).

As Gass makes the distinction, it is essentially one of quality. Great works of literature have authors; other, ordinary uses of speech and writing, including bad literature, have no author. And Gass is willing to follow Gertrude Stein in a similar distinction between "human nature" and "the human mind." Human nature is the writer's physical identity in time and space, while the human mind is "a universal level of creativity and thought" (285). Gass's use of Stein's distinction, like his use of the writer/author distinction, separates work on the basis of quality: "Every author has an identity, but masterpieces are written by the human mind, not by human nature, which only lends them their common smell and color, their day-to-day dust." Barthes, according to Gass, is not announcing just the death of "every author" of the common human nature variety, but he is announcing the death of the human mind as author. Against this, Gass argues that the human mind, whenever it is incarnate in "a self which is so certain of its spirit and so insistent on its presence that it puts itself in its syllables like Mr. Gorgeous in his shimmering gown" (287), is immortal. It has not died, and it will not. The human mind confronts us, it refuses to flatter or serve, it "is a bother to us"; but "that is why we need authors: they re-fuse. Readers, on the other hand . . . readers . . . readers simply comprise the public" (288).

Gass's last-second insult against his audience is a vivid illustration of the difference between his essay and Barthes's. Barthes argues for a complete separation of the creative author (the "Author") and the created author (the "scriptor"). This allows him to remove all control over the meaning of the text from the creative author and give it over wholly into the hands of the reader. Gass, conversely, argues for an identity between the creative author (the "historical author") and the created author (the "artificial author"), or at least that the creative author is creator, sustainer, and lord of the created author, which allows him to give complete control over the meaning of the text into the hands of the creative author, and to remove all power from the reader. Barthes, in other words, denies that writing is creative, while Gass denies that reading is creative.

54

Barthes insists on each of the following claims: (1) There is a difference between creative author and created author. His terms, of course, are "Author" and "scriptor." The Author is "the past of his own book," while the scriptor "is born simultaneously with the text" at each reading (not at the time of the text's composition). (2) The writer does not create the text. Although the Author (whom I am calling the creative author) is the past of his own book, he does not create it, at least not in the sense of bringing forth something whose origin is himself. Instead, he merely "imitate[s] a gesture which is always anterior," he "mix[es] writings"; he is "a multi-dimensional space in which a variety of writings, none of them original, blend and clash." (3) The writer is never present in the text. He has been "removed" from the text by the nature of writing itself, since it is "the destruction of every voice, of every point of origin." (4) The Author has no relationship to the scriptor, who is created wholly by the act of reading. The Author has no role in the creation of the scriptor, because "only language acts," only language creates the text, not the Author. The text is written when it is read (and *only* when it is read), and the scriptor is born with the text at each reading. The only conclusion compatible with these four claims is that any similarity between the creative author and the created author is entirely circumstantial, not based on causation and certainly not based on identity; and that the reader wholly determines the meaning of the text.

By contrast, Gass asserts: (1) There is, true enough, a difference between the creative author and the created author. The "poet of the poem" is not a historical person in the same way that the "real" poet is. (2) The writer is eternally present in the text. Gass is not even willing to admit that there is any question about this issue: The only question is whether the text will by itself interest us in the writer, not whether the writer "is present in the work in one way or another." (3) The writer brings *himself* to life in the text. Gass implies this throughout "The Death of the Author" with his talk of poems "infused with the poet's presence" and of authors "appear[ing] on page after page," but he has argued for the same claim at greater length already in "The Soul Inside the Sentence." Any text that is authored is not merely a sign of the existence somewhere of a soul, but itself has a soul, the transmigrated soul of its author: When someone like Thomas Browne wrote a masterpiece, he "did not merely bring these books of his, these eloquent passages, their memorable lines, into being; *he brought himself into existence on the page,* as it were through a hole in the word" (1986b, 140). This is the crux of the dispute. It is *because* the creative author is *un*able to transubstantiate himself that when the text is finished, "when the act of writing is done," the Author for Barthes is dead. Someone is born at each reading, but it is not a rebirth, it is not the Author who is born. Similarly, it is *because* the creative author is *able* to re-create himself within the text that on Gass's view the author is alive and well. (4) The creative author and the created author are one and the same. Gass has admitted already that one is historical and one is transhistorical, but the operative metaphor through the essay is immortality, and in the Christian view the same is true of the earthly and heavenly lives of men. "The same" here must be taken to mean the maintenance of a singular identity through a change in form. The Jesus Christ who is now seated at the right hand of the Father is the same Jesus who was crucified; and the Thomas Browne who is present in *Urn-Burial* is the same Thomas Browne who lived from 1605 to 1682 and wrote that book as well as others, like *Religio Medici*. The only conclusion compatible with Gass's four premises is that the created author is continuous with and wholly determined by the creative author; and that the writer wholly determines the meaning of the text, while the reader is only a passive receiver of that meaning.

The two positions, however, are equally extreme. The fact that the work is produced through the manipulation of language rather than being created *ex nihilo,* and that the text, once finished, separates itself from the writer, is no reason to believe with Barthes that in writing "all identity is lost." Yet the fact that some historical individual stood at the origin of a text is no reason to believe with Gass that the identity that results from a reading of that text is in every case the identity of the person who originally composed the text. Instead, as I will argue at length in later chapters, it is more accurate and more useful to begin with the recognition that the relationships between authors, their texts, and the readers of their texts vary greatly, and that there is always a mutual interdependence. It is true that as soon as the creative act is over, the writer herself is removed from the text ("dead") in the sense that she is no longer exerting active influence over its meaning, but it is not true that the writer is removed in the sense that the influence she exerted in the creative act is nullified or discontinued.

Since Barthes and Gass both see the question of the death of the author as a theological question, it is fitting to conclude with an evaluation of their views in comparison to traditional religious notions. Erich Frank has argued in *Philosophical Understanding and Religious Truth* that in religion the ideas of creation, time, and immortality are intimately linked. The traditional Christian notion of creation *ex nihilo,* "the bringing forth of something out of nothing, absolute origination," was, Frank says, "utterly foreign to Greek philosophy" (1982, 58). For the Greeks, the world "had its beginning in itself. It had sprung from an original state, chaos or matter, which in somewhat changed form, as its true 'nature,' remained inherent in it." Thus, time for the Greeks was the time of nature, a circle based on the revolutions of the heavenly bodies and the cycles of nature, and human immortality was within that circular framework: For the Greeks, the human soul is "drawn back again into the life-cycle, into a new body" (67). But with the Christian idea of creation came a new view of time, in which man "sees himself as a unique, unrepeatable individuality" without a past but with a future. Time to the Christian is "a straight line which leads into the future towards a definite goal" (68). Greek man had "no definite aim, no real future," only a past; the past of Christian man "fades into a mere shadow," leaving him with only a future.

Using Frank's synopsis as the basis for the analogy, and substituting the author for God (or the gods) and the text for man, Gass's view might be described as a "Christian" view of textual history, and Barthes's view as a "Greek" view of textual history. For Gass, although of course the author is limited to what Frank calls "production" since he cannot create the text, as God did the world, *ex nihilo*, the author is in God's image in at least this respect: He controls the shape of his "creation" by imposition of his will, and the creation that results embodies its creator in such a way that no one could fail to see him in his handiwork. The text is a "unique, unrepeatable individuality" with a distinct origin and a linear history. But just as Nietzsche, in order to oppose the Christian view of creation, "tried to revive the ancient concept of the circular movement of time and of the eternal recurrence of the same events" (Frank 1982, 68), so Barthes, in order to oppose the "Christian" view of textual history, revives the ancient concept of cyclical time. The Greek gods did not stand at the origin of time and the world, nor did they "invade" time and the world from without; instead, they were themselves within the circle of time. Similarly, for Barthes, the author does not stand at the origin of the work, but is herself caught up within it. The text is not a "unique, unrepeatable individuality," but a result of the forces of language, into which it is absorbed again to be reborn, like the Greek soul, in another body. Gass's textual eternity, like the Christian eternity, is "absolute timelessness, something beyond time and incommensurable with it" (Frank 1982, 60), in which the text is created by "the human mind," a transcendental entity that operates in the Kantian noumenal world; and in which the text, once created, is endowed with an eternal soul. Barthes's textual eternity, on the other hand, is, like the Greek eternity, "an everlasting now, a perpetual present" (Frank 1982, 60), in which the text "is eternally written here and now" (Barthes 1977, 145).

But if my analyses of Barthes and Gass in this chapter and my arguments in the book as a whole are successful, they will show that neither the "Christian" view espoused by Gass nor the "Greek" view espoused by Barthes is wholly accurate; that, in other words, the author in her relationship to the text is strictly analogous neither to the Christian God in his relationship to his creation nor to the Greek gods in their relationship to the world. Whether or not Erich Frank is correct in his claim that, as regards our understanding of the world, a given view of time is possible only on a certain view of creation, it is not true that, as regards our understanding of texts, a view of "textual creation" corresponding to a certain view of the creation of the world need be accompanied by a view of "textual time" or of "authorial immortality" corresponding to the view of "earthly time" or of "human immortality" that accompanies the given view of the earth's creation. The fact that there is a unique, unrepeatable author (the creative author) who is in at least some sense a master of language and who stands at the temporal origin of a text does not mean that there is no (created) author who is eternally produced by the language of the text; the fact that some "soul" (the created author) is immortal in the work does not mean that it is the soul of the "unique, unrepeatable person" (the creative author) who wrote the work; and the fact that the creative author, like Frank's Greek man, has only a past does not mean that the text (and the created author with it) does not have a future.

CHAPTER 4

Et Alii

The last pair of "characters in search of an author" will actually be not a pair of characters at all, but several of them. So far I have reacted to the two most imposing debates on authorship; in this chapter, I will consider (in a form something like an omnibus review) several minor statements about authorship, each a preparation for, a reaction to, or an evaluation of, one or more of the interlocutors in the two primary debates.

New Critics' Critics

The first chapter of E. D. Hirsch's *Validity in Interpretation* is entitled "In Defense of the Author," but the author Hirsch defends is a gaunt one. Hirsch tries to protect this author against four claims championed by the New Critics: (1) The meaning of a text changes—even for the author, (2) it does not matter what an author means—only what his text says, (3) the author's meaning is inaccessible, and (4) the author often does not know what he means. In each case, Hirsch's objective is to show that what the author intended is the correct meaning of the text. And in each case, he assumes without argument that there is a single correct meaning for every text. Nehamas argued for critical monism; Hirsch assumes its truth without argument.

The emaciation of the author Hirsch wishes to defend is depicted most graphically in the section concerned with the inaccessibility of the author's meaning. Hirsch holds a view about authors' methods of creation that only a "critic" and not a "real writer" could hold. He assumes that, although an author may have in mind many meanings while he is writing (1967, 17), he can mean only one thing by what he wrote (8). An author, on Hirsch's view, recognizing that words can handle only one meaning at a time, tries to pin them down to the one meaning that she wants. The successful reader will then ascertain the meaning to which the author wished to pin the words. But one need only read Wallace Stevens's *The Necessary Angel* or Louis Zukofsky's *Prepositions* to realize that at least some authors have a different method and a different view. It is also possible to believe that words can handle more meanings than we can, and that the power of language is not exhausted by attempting to restrict it to a single meaning. Poets like Stevens and Zukofsky aim not to narrow language but to tap into its power, not to set up a simple circuit but to touch live wires and watch the sparks fly. Hirsch writes that "it is altogether likely that no text can ever convey all the meanings an author had in mind as he wrote" (17), but what someone like Stevens would say is that it is altogether likely that no author can have in mind all the meanings his texts convey.

Ultimately, though, the problem with Hirsch's view is not his mistaken belief about the act of writing; it is that in consequence of that belief his view of interpretation is impoverished. Like the writing of texts, "the interpretation of texts is concerned exclusively with sharable meanings" (18), according to Hirsch. An author may have many meanings, but he tries to convey only one of them through the text; the reader may see many meanings in the text, but she is concerned with only the one meaning the author tried to convey. But like authors, readers are not all as hollow as those on which Hirsch's ideas are contingent. If interpretation consists only in the attempt to discover what the author meant, then interpretation is a very minor part of reading. If the author can have in mind more meanings than he can share with the reader, then surely it is true of any serious and resourceful reader that she can receive from the text more meanings than she can share with the author. In other words, the real problem with Hirsch's view is that, given his distinction between "a man's meaning and his subject matter" (20), he does not recognize that what he calls "subject matter" is the more important of the two.

J. Timothy Bagwell, in his *American Formalism and the Problem of Interpretation*, offers a lucid and thorough analysis not only of the New Critical groundwork of Wimsatt and Beardsley, but also of Hirsch's relation to this groundwork. Bagwell argues that the entire debate about intention depends on the question of whether literary discourse works in the same way ordinary discourse works. In ordinary discourse, Bagwell says, "getting back to the author's intention is [always] the cognitive goal" (1986, 15), and the actual utterance is only a tool toward that end. What counts is "not what an utterance means but what the speaker imputes it to mean" (91). For example,

> If someone says to me, "You came home late last night," and I reply, "What is that supposed to mean?," I will probably accept the speaker's expressed intention—to express concern, to scold, and so forth—as determining the operative meaning of the utterance because it is the intention that concerns me." (14–15)

For this reason, "if literary meaning is continuous with ordinary communication, then the question [of whether the author's

63

intentions are relevant] does not arise" (15). Wimsatt and Beardsley believe that literary discourse is not continuous with ordinary discourse, and try to "defend literary meaning against the vagaries of intentionalist speculation" (99); Hirsch believes that literary meaning is continuous with ordinary discourse, and tries to defend meaning in general, and especially meaning in literary discourse, "against the vagaries of speculative interpretation" (99). Bagwell believes that literary discourse is not continuous with ordinary discourse, and tries to defend against mistaking one for the other. He asks how to tell when a verbal intention is a literary intention, or "when is a verbal intention immune to the claim of other verbal intentions?" (89). The latter question is Bagwell's answer to the former. A verbal intention is a literary intention when it is immune to the claims of other verbal intentions. A work is literature when it "is something which is to be understood rather than explicated" (102), that is, when no other verbal intentions can adjudicate its claims.

Yet in spite of the light it sheds on Wimsatt, Beardsley, Hirsch (and Stanley Fish), Bagwell's argument is based on a false premise. Hidden behind his assumption that literary discourse is not continuous with ordinary discourse (and that everything is either one or the other) is the unstated assumption that all literary discourse works in the same way and all ordinary discourse works in the same way. But not all discourse is clearly "literary" or clearly "ordinary." If an eminent Shakespeare scholar, having been served a burned steak at a restaurant and having been refused in her request for a properly cooked one, says to her waiter in rage, "Thy food is such as hath been belch'd on by infected lungs," her utterance is not clearly in either of Bagwell's categories. If the scholar were asked (a week later) if her comment was literary discourse, she no doubt would say that it was. If the waiter were asked whether the comment was ordinary discourse, he no doubt would say that it was not. Yet it had the property of imputed meaning being dominant, which Bagwell says is characteristic of ordinary discourse. And not all literary discourse works in the same way. When Shakespeare in *Pericles* has Marina say "thy food is such / As hath been belch'd on by infected lungs," his discourse does not seem to be working in precisely the same way (i.e., does not stand in the same relation to its author's intentions) as when Nietzsche has Zarathustra say, "You look up when you feel the need for elevation. And I look down because I am elevated." In one case, it is unlikely that the character is in any direct sense speaking for the author; in the other, whether the character is in any sense speaking for the author is at least problematic. One purpose of the extended argument of this book is to move beyond the false dilemma of attempting to describe two domains that are mutually exclusive and internally homogeneous.

William E. Cain

William E. Cain's "Authors and Authority in Interpretation" is a reaction largely to two opposed views, those of Foucault and Hirsch. Cain is concerned with the *consequences* of views about authors; specifically, he wants to know whether and how structuralist/deconstructive views of the author undermine authority, and how responsibility on the part of the author and the reader can be maintained in the face of this challenge to authority. Given that "theorists have called into question terms like author, reader, and text, and attacked the notion of stable, verifiable meanings," Cain wants to know how "we" (his assumed audience is English professors) "justify what we do" (1980, 618). I will isolate three of his claims in particular, disagreeing with two of them and agreeing with the other.

The first claim occurs in a discussion of Wimsatt and Beardsley's "The Intentional Fallacy." Cain argues that, even though Wimsatt and Beardsley remove the author's intention as a criterion for evaluating and interpreting a work, they still let the author return to the text "by the back door" (622). They still talk, Cain says, as if someone were doing for the text what they will not permit the author to do, like " 'handl[ing]' a poem's 'complex of meaning' " and " 'exclud[ing]' irrelevancies" (622); they simply avoid, by means of the passive voice, the question of who is doing the author's old job. Cain says Wimsatt and Beardsley cannot be right, because someone must be actively imposing design on the text, someone must be doing the text's intending, "someone must be smoothing out the lumps in the pudding and getting the bugs out of the machinery" (622).

My objection is not simply that this is an *undefended* assumption, but that it is a *mistaken* one. Wimsatt and Beardsley's error may be hidden behind the passive voice; Cain's is hidden behind the present tense. Even if one accepts the analogy of author as chef/text as pudding, there is no reason to believe that the author's action is a perpetually present one. A chef, after all, does not follow his pudding to the table; he tries to get any lumps out before giving it to the waiter. If the customer gets smooth pudding, it is not because of what the chef *is doing*, but because of what the chef *has done*. Someone must have smoothed out the lumps in the pudding, but no one need be presently smoothing out the lumps. And the author as mechanic/text as machine analogy is, I think, a bad one, because the laws of physics do not hold for works of literature. Sears makes more money in a day selling maintenance agreements on Craftsman lawnmowers and Kenmore washers than you or I will make in a lifetime, precisely because machines break down. They need not only someone to operate them, but also someone to maintain them. However, there is no a priori reason to believe that texts, if they are machines, cannot be self-propelled, maintenance-free, perpetual-motion machines. Cain does not exclude the possibility that more than one person may be involved in the design, production, operation, and maintenance of the textual machine: Lee Iacocca may have thought up the 7/70 protection plan and be making a killing off of it, but don't expect to see him in greasy coveralls, socket wrench in hand, balanced on his belly on the radiator of a LeBaron. Cain does assume, though, that the agent controlling the text must be perpetually penetrating the text from outside.

The alternative Cain ignores (and one of the theses I am arguing for in this book) is that the text can maintain itself. Once the work has been made, we may talk (and *do* talk) of an agent influencing the text with intentions, meanings, and so on; that agent, though, is not the cause of the text but its result, not perpetually penetrating the text from outside but sending out its energy from within the text. The text, in other words, does not need external authority to have authority.

My agreement with Cain is on a similar claim. He isolates a mistaken assumption shared by Hirsch, M. H. Abrams, and other "defenders of the faith" in their arguments against Foucault and the rest of the "French connection." The mistaken assumption is that "we must agree to honor an absolute authority, or else undermine our interpretive work and our institutions" (628). Cain says against this that (1) "Foucault does not argue that authority should (or could) be made to disappear entirely," (2) Foucault in fact "describe[s] the different kinds of authority the term [author] manifests," and (3) the academic institution's ability to assimilate radical ideas is greater than the power of ideas to destroy the institution, so that even revolutionary theories about the author are not the sort of threat to "us" that Hirsch et al. fear they are (628).

One might supplement Cain's refutation of the mistaken assumption made by Hirsch et al. by appealing to similar challenges to authority in the past. Darwin is an easy example. The paradigmatic pre-Darwin view of nature, that of William Paley, is similar to the traditional view of the text. Paley believes that "contrivance . . . proves the *personality* of the Deity" because no animal "can have been the author to itself of the design with which they were constructed [*sic*]" (1854, 462–63). The order of the world implies the activity of a rational agent penetrating nature from outside. Darwin took the same type of phenomena to which Paley appeals (the eyes of fishes for one, the tails and crops of domestic pigeons for the other), but he drew a different inference, powerful for its parsimony. Darwin argued that one need not posit agency outside nature to account for nature. Defenders of the traditional view used an argument not altogether unlike the summary of Hirsch's argument in Cain: Darwin's view is wrong because it threatens authority. But what was actually the case with Darwin's opponents was not that authority per se was threatened, but that *their* authority was threatened. Darwin was not eliminating authority from nature, but he was relocating authority within nature and, in the process, eliminating the authority on which his opponents depended. Cain correctly observes that Foucault et al. do not threaten to eliminate authority from texts; but they do relocate authority within the text (or reader), and in the process eliminate the authority on which Hirsch et al. depend. The question is not whether there is agency or authority in texts; the question is where that authority is to be found, and in what it actually resides. Foucault, Barthes, and their affiliates will not be satisfied by an appeal to tradition ("But we've always believed that authority comes from authors"), nor by the pragmatic response Cain attributes to Hirsch ("But we need this authority or we'll be out of a job"). They do not want to know where we have always thought authority lay, or where we would like for it to come from; they want to know where it really is. Ironically, the ones accused of forsaking truth appear in this case to be the ones most hotly in pursuit of it, and the self-proclaimed defenders of truth seem to be the ones guilty of the same slippery-slope argument to which Darwin's opponents appealed: If *our* authority is undermined, *all* authority will be.

My second disagreement with Cain has to do with a reservation he expresses. Having argued in favor of Foucault's view over Hirsch's, Cain begins the fourth and last section of his paper by saying that although he agrees with much Foucault says, yet "I do not want to displace altogether the values of personal responsibility, self-awareness, and self-consciousness about what one writes" (631). Surely no humanist, not even Barthes, Foucault, or Derrida, wishes to displace such values. The fear that such values will be displaced as a result of Foucault's analysis of the author (or any similar analysis) is, I think, ungrounded for the same reasons that Hirsch's fear that certain views about authors undercut all authority is ungrounded, and for the same reasons that a Christian's fear that disbelief in God will remove an individual's ethical responsibility is ungrounded.

One reason that Cain's fear is ungrounded is that Foucault's essay on the author is strictly from the viewpoint of the reader of a text, and is concerned with what the reader is to do about the text, not what the writer is to do. In fact, Foucault, as discussed in the previous chapter, distinguishes between the writer and the author, and specifically says he is talking about the writer and not the author. Cain gives no reason to believe that the change in an author's status in relation to the text after its creation results in a concomitant change in the writer's status in relation to the text before its creation, and I suggest that there *is* no reason to believe that.

69

A second reason that Cain's fear is ungrounded is that it is really a specific instance of Glaucon's fear from Book 2 of the *Republic*. Glaucon argues that if there were no threat of punishment, everyone would pursue his own self-interest with complete disregard for others; Socrates argues, against Glaucon's view, that there are other reasons, besides fear of punishment, to be good. Similarly, Cain, even though he recognizes that there is no need to fear loss of authority when the author's status is revised, seems to believe that there is reason to fear loss of responsibility. I contend that there are reasons, besides the belief that one is "freely creative" (631) or that one will exert a perpetual influence over the text, to be responsible, self-aware, and self-conscious about what one writes. Even in the worst scenario, if the text is utterly disconnected from the writer after it has been created, if she will suffer no consequences and receive no benefits from it for better or worse, and if she has no interpretive influence whatever once it leaves her word processor, there is still reason not to "displace altogether the values" Cain advocates.

If there are any ethical consequences from a change in our understanding of the author, it seems to me that they are positive consequences. They would amount to a change from a concern for responsibility (with all its questions of "to whom?" and "for what?") to a concern for integrity. If the author's death were in any (obviously metaphorical) sense also the writer's death, the stakes would be even higher than before. Then to write would always be to risk one's life; then one would write only because he didn't understand the risk involved, or because he had to, because he was abiding by what Lynne McFall in an essay on integrity calls the "Olaf Principle":[1] "There are some things that one is not prepared to do, or some things one must do" (1987, 11), even if it means suffering or death.

Robert Stecker

If Cain's article is the anxious analysis of one who recognizes the import of the various recent attempts to revise critical understanding of the author, Robert Stecker's "Apparent, Implied, and Postulated Authors" is the impatient complaint of one who doesn't understand what all the fuss is about. We already have a writer and a narrator, and three's a crowd. Stecker wants to know why the apparent (Kendall Walton), implied (Wayne Booth), or postulated (Alexander Nehamas) author is necessary.

One might object to the question itself. Stecker's own formulation of his concern is this: "What motivates making this further distinction [between a writer and an apparent, implied, or postulated author]? Does the motivation justify the distinction, i.e. establish that there really is a need for it? These are the questions I want to answer" (1987, 258). The suggestion is that the issue is strictly a pragmatic one: We have been getting along just fine without this tertium quid, so why not leave well enough alone? It does not appear to matter to Stecker whether in leaving well enough alone we are parsimoniously prohibiting the appearance of some false, imaginary character, or whether we are ignoring something that in fact is active in the text. The same defense could be used to defend belief in a flat earth. But this may be to judge the essay too hastily.

One might also object that Stecker's essay ignores the problems raised by a now fairly substantial body of philosophical opposition to the Cartesian subject. One might say of these problems what Basil Bunting says of Pound's *Cantos:* "You will have to go a long way round / if you want to avoid them." Stecker's argument does avoid them, depending as it does on the assumption that an author is a Cartesian subject, one who thinks, intends, and so on, and whose actions (like writing) and the resultant objects (like texts) preserve her identity. Stecker is willing to go "a long way round" Wittgenstein's *Tractatus* 5.631, for example, which denies that assumption.

> There is no such thing as the subject that thinks or entertains ideas.
> If I wrote a book called *The World as I found it*, I should have to include a report on my body, and should have to say which parts were subordinate to my will, and which were not, etc., this being a method of isolating the subject, or rather of showing that in an important sense there is no subject; for it alone could *not* be mentioned in that book.—

But to expect the essay to solve that problem may be to ask it to do too much.

It is not too much, though, to expect an argument that does not beg the question, and Stecker's argument fails on that count. Here is Stecker's statement, on the second page of his essay, of the two alternatives in evaluating Kendall Walton's apparent author:

> If we are concerned with appearances simply as our initial estimate of reality and if the focus of critical inquiry is the way a work really is, the intentions an artist really had, etc., then Walton's usage will prove more cumbersome than useful. On the other hand, if the focus of critical inquiry is or ought to be the appearances themselves, then Walton's usage will help us to maintain that focus and not confuse it with the alternative just mentioned. (259)

The terms "appearance" and "reality," in which this tendentious statement of alternatives is framed, are loaded terms.[2] The second alternative, as it is formulated here, is obviously not a live option: No one will be content with mere appearance when presented with the alternative of getting past appearance to reality. But the question of whether one needs the "apparent author" is just the question of whether the appearance of the text is "mere appearance" or whether it *is* reality. Stecker simply gives the problem in such a way that his answer is already implied in his formulation of the question. He is assuming that the past (what the artist did) is real, and that the present (what the text and reader are doing) is "merely" apparent. He is assuming just the "metaphors of depth and uncovering" against which Nehamas argues so forcefully.

This leads to a number of mistakes on Stecker's part, but one illustration should suffice. On pages 259–60, responding to a passage in which Walton asks one to imagine that a computer, rather than T. S. Eliot, wrote "The Love Song of J. Alfred Prufrock," Stecker replies simply that "though [such] possibilities are conceivable, they are not possibilities we have to dispose of before attributing the act of [portraying the hero compassionately] to Eliot because none of these are possibilities there is any reason to take seriously. We know who wrote 'Prufrock' so we can take for granted that the words of the poem are evidence of his acts and intentions" (260). There are two reasons why this is an oversimplification. First, I will give examples in a later chapter of problem cases in which we know who wrote a work, but cannot take for granted that it is evidence of his intentions: Numerous ancient texts and religious texts, for example, claim to be inspired, that is, to be evidence of the intentions of someone or something other than the person who wrote the text, and even a person who disbelieves all such claims cannot simply take for granted that they are false. Second, even if we did know that "the words of the poem are evidence of [the writer's] acts and intentions," we still would not know what *kind* of evidence they are. Are we to take Prufrock's question "Shall I part my hair behind?" as evidence that Eliot had begun to grow bald by the time he composed "Prufrock," or that he was worried about someday being bald, or that he sympathized with bald men even though from knowledge of his mother's family he knew he himself would never be bald?

At bottom, I believe that Stecker's disagreement with Walton, Nehamas, and Booth is largely verbal. Walton, Nehamas, and Booth start with the admission that a "real" writer's "real" intentions are at the least difficult (and maybe impossible) to ascertain, and the belief that in consequence of that the person whose intentions we debate when interpreting a work is not the "real" writer. Stecker says this person is the "real" writer, but he gives evidence that he is talking about the same person the others say is not the "real" writer when (at p. 267) he agrees with Nehamas that a writer "is doing" something "in a work," in spite of the fact that most "real" writers are dead and none are doing things in texts at the time readers other than themselves are interpreting. The "real" writer *did* something; the "apparent" or "implied" or "postulated" author *is doing* something. Further, Stecker softens his position at the end of his essay. He concludes that it may be useful for "special cases" in fields other than literature (as if works of art were not all special cases), but that "whether the notion of apparent artist has any useful application to literature . . . I do not know" (270). He does not want to deny that apparent authors may be important, but he himself cannot "find room for the apparent author between the narrator and the real author" (267). If the observation that the author Stecker describes as currently active in the work and to whom he ascribes intentions is not the "real" historical writer is insufficient persuasion that there is someone between the narrator and the "real author," one might point to examples like those in the later chapter on the created author, in which the narrator and "real author," even if one believed in his perpetual effect on the text, are not enough to account for all the intentions we infer.

Jacques Derrida

Jacques Derrida's position concerning the author, in spite of the metonymic form of expression it receives, adds little to Barthes's position. The similarity of his position to Barthes's is not surprising, given the similarity of their views about writing. I quoted this passage from Barthes above: "Writing is the destruction of every voice, of every point of origin. Writing is that neutral, composite, oblique space where our subject slips away, the negative where all identity is lost, starting with the very identity of the body writing" (1977, 142). It has this double in Derrida:

> From the moment that the proper name is erased in a
> system, there is writing. . . . If writing is no longer
> understood in the narrow sense of linear and phonetic
> notation, it should be possible to say that all societies
> capable of producing, that is to say of obliterating, their
> proper names . . . practice writing in general. (1976, 108–9)

He writes later in the same book of "literary suicide," of "death by writing" (142–43), in which presence is replaced by value; again strikingly similar to Barthes.

When Derrida directly addresses authorship (no postal pun intended, if such a lack of intention matters, or if such a disavowal of intention can be believed) he does so metonymically, by talking about the signature, most notably in two essays,

"Signature Event Context" and "Interpreting Signatures (Nietzsche/ Heidegger): Two Questions." In the former, Derrida asks whether "writing" is a phenomenon within the presumably larger category of "communication," and he resolves this question into the question of whether the context of a writing imposes limits on it. Derrida attempts to render problematic the concepts of communication and context, so he does not define or enclose either term, but he does answer the question that is relevant here. The author is part of the context that is usually taken to impose limits on a text: His personal circumstances at the time of writing, his intentions, and so on, help to determine the meaning of a text. But if it is not clear what Derrida thinks "context" is or whether these things are part of "context," it *is* clear that Derrida says that they impose no constraints on the text.

What distinguishes writing from speech, and what frees it from context, is its "iterability." One writes while the one written to is absent, and the writing continues to be legible even after the individual(s) addressed is dead (1972, 315). Writing also continues to be legible in the writer's absence.

> To write is to produce a mark that will constitute a kind of machine that is in turn productive, that my future disappearance in principle will not prevent from functioning and from yielding, and yielding itself to, reading and rewriting. . . . For the written to be the written, it must continue to "act" and to be legible even if what is called the author of the writing no longer answers for what he has written, for what he seems to have signed, whether he is provisionally absent, or if he is dead, or if in general he does not support, with his absolutely current and present intention or attention, the plenitude of his

meaning, of that very thing which seems to be written "in
his name." (316)

This means that if for Hirsch "meaning is an affair of consciousness" (1967, 23), for Derrida writing is "cut off . . . from *consciousness* as the authority of the last analysis" (316). Derrida's
metaphor for the author's relation to the text is an indirect
version of Barthes's: Barthes says the author is dead, Derrida
says the text is "orphaned, and separated at birth from the
assistance of its father" (316). All the criticisms of Barthes's
view apply to Derrida's as well.

"Interpreting Signatures" appears at first to be as indebted
to Foucault as "Signature Event Context" is to Barthes. Foucault argues that the author has served traditionally as "a [re-
pressive] principle of unity in writing" (1977, 128), and Derrida,
following Heidegger, starts by thinking of the author's proper
name "not as that of an individual or that of a signatory; it is
the name of a thought, of a thought whose *unity* gives in return
sense and reference to the proper name" (1986, 250; my emphasis). Foucault's analysis of the traditional view (which he opposes) is that it takes the author's name as giving unity to texts;
Derrida's Heideggerian starting point is that the texts give unity
to the name. But the essay is neither as derivative nor as sterile
as at first it seems, for immediately after the passage I have just
quoted he identifies two alternatives that result from starting
with this view of the author's proper name: (1) Take "a new
approach to the problematic of the name," and (2) determine
the content of the name from the thought with which it is
associated. To take the latter alternative is "to let fall into
inessentiality the particular proper name, which has become
the index of the 'biography' or a 'psychology' of an individual"
(250), to let the particular proper name drop out. But to take the
first alternative is to "risk . . . seeing the name dismembered

and multiplied in masks and similitudes." Although Derrida does not draw out all the implications of this alternative, it is not for that reason less fecund. He does observe that "since Aristotle, and at least up until Bergson, 'it' (metaphysics) has constantly repeated and assumed that to think and to say must mean to think and say something that would be a *one*, one *matter*" (257). Derrida's objection to this assumption, and the one I wish to follow through on, he formulates in this way: "But who ever has said that a person bears a single name?" (256). If the author does *not* bear a single name, if the author's name is "dismembered and multiplied in masks and similitudes," then what are the names and how do they function, and what are the masks and likenesses? If the author is not one but many, then who is he (are they)? It is questions like these that I will explore in what follows.

TWO

The Creative Author

Now he is scattered among a hundred cities
And wholly given over to unfamiliar affections,
To find his happiness in another kind of wood
And be punished under a foreign code of conscience.
The words of a dead man
Are modified in the guts of the living.

—W. H. Auden

An investigation into human creativity and creation is apt to have one of two primary concerns: either a "psychological" concern or a "technical" concern. The psychological concern asks such questions as "What makes one person more creative than another?" and "What psychological factors account for the production of great works of art?" The technical concern, on the other hand, asks about the process of creation: "What occurs in an act of artistic creation?" The former is concerned with the creative agent and the latter with the creative act; in that sense the two concerns may be thought of as parallel to the common division of ethics into agent-centered ethics and act-centered ethics. And the analogy may be carried one step further, since in neither case (the investigation of creation, the investigation of ethics) can concern for either agent or act be considered to the complete exclusion of the other. One cannot decide whether a given action is good without at least addressing the issue of whether the agent's intentions weigh in the evaluation of the action; and one cannot decide whether a certain individual is a good person without at least addressing the issue of whether the quality of her actions should weigh in the evaluation of her goodness. Similarly, one cannot discuss creative agents without reference to creative acts, nor can one discuss creative acts without reference to creative agents.

The case, then, with the psychological and technical concerns in the study of creation is the same as with sound and thought in Saussure's study of linguistics: They may be compared with a sheet of paper, one concern being the front of the sheet and the other the back; and "one cannot cut the front without cutting the back at the same time" (Saussure 1966, 113). Most studies of creation and creativity have looked at the front, the psychological concern, while cutting the sheet, but I want to look at the other side, the technical concern. I will propose as a heuristic device a model of the creative process that will make it possible to account not only for typical cases of artistic production but also for problematic cases of authorship such as the Homeric poems.

Kenneth Burke's *A Grammar of Motives* begins with five terms (act, scene, agent, agency, purpose) that "generate" his investigation into motives. His terms are variables that a description of motives must specify in order to be complete. Although the nature of my inquiry is different, I will begin with five terms that are not wholly disanalogous to Burke's. They are ore, arché, archive, artisan, and artifact. Like Burke's terms, these are variables that a description of a creative act must specify in order to be complete.

To sketch the meaning of the terms, consider the creation of a literary work (as compared to, say, a sculpture). The *ore* is the raw materials that are conditions for the possibility of the creation of the work, and might include, though it would not be limited to: the tradition out of which the work arises, for instance, the pastoral tradition out of which "Lycidas" arises; the language in which the work is written; and historical events the work incorporates into its narrative. The *arché* is the source of or the inspiration for the work; it is that to which or to whom the work is attributed. For instance, in the epic tradition the arché is usually personified as the Muses, while in the case of Scripture it is normally the deity who is thought of as the arché. The *archive* is the "true work" given by the arché, whose essence the artisan tries to capture in the written text he produces. The *artisan* generally can be identified with the historical person who has produced the artifact (though, as will become clear later, this is not always so), and when this identification holds is commonly referred to as the author or writer. The *artifact* is the work itself.

CHAPTER 5

Five Modes of Creation

N orthrop Frye begins the first essay in his *Anatomy of Criticism* by outlining a classification of fictions into five modes based on the hero's power of action. The first mode is the *mythic* mode, in which the hero is a divine being, "superior in *kind* both to other men and to the environment of other men" (1957, 33). The second mode is the *romantic* mode, in which the hero is superior not in kind but in degree to other men and to his environment. His "actions are marvelous but [he] is himself identified as a human being"; he "moves in a world in which the ordinary laws of nature are slightly suspended." The third mode is the *high mimetic* mode, in which the hero is a leader, "superior in degree to other men but not to his natural environment. . . . He has authority, passions, and powers of expression far greater than ours, but what he does is subject both to social criticism and to the order of nature" (33–34). Most epic and tragedy is in the high mimetic mode. The fourth mode is the *low mimetic* mode, in which the hero is one of us, "superior neither to other men nor to his environment." In this mode, the mode of most comedy and of realistic fiction, "we respond to a sense of [the hero's] common humanity, and demand from the poet the same canons of probability that we find in our own experience." The fifth and final mode is the *ironic* mode. In this mode, the hero is "inferior in power or intelligence to ourselves, so that we have the sense of looking down on a scene of bondage, frustration, or absurdity." Frye's classification is intended to elucidate the relations between genres and their significance in our understanding of literature. According to Frye, "European fiction, during the last fifteen centuries, has steadily moved its center of gravity down the list" (34).

In this chapter I will construct a classification that, though similar in spirit, is based not on the hero's role in the fiction, but on the artisan's supposed role in the creative process. There have been many and various attempts to understand and explain the general creative ability shared by all humans and the creative genius possessed by extraordinary artists, writers, musicians, and scientists. This classification of creative modes is intended not simply to offer yet another explanation, but to identify and explore the conceptual pattern behind the historical variations. There is, though, a procedural difficulty in the path of a classification of creative modes that does not similarly obstruct Frye's classification of fictional modes. The difficulty is this. The hero's power of action should be determinable strictly on the basis of the work itself. Even in a controversial case (for instance, Satan in *Paradise Lost*) the evidence for each side of the controversy will be drawn from within the work. But the artisan's supposed role in the creative process is not as easy to determine as the hero's power of action; it is more likely to be controversial; and the evidence for it is not always contained within the work. For what determines the artisan's supposed role in the creative process is not the story the work itself provides, which normally is relatively "stable," but the story told *about* the work, which is more likely to fall predominantly under the control of historians, critics, and readers, and therefore to be subject to wider variation. Were it possible to

visit the underworld with a copy of St. Luke's Gospel and *Anatomy of Criticism*, probably one could persuade St. Augustine
and Friedrich Nietzsche to agree on the hero's power of action
in that Gospel, and so to agree on the fictional mode to which
it belongs; but probably one could not persuade them to agree
about the artisan's role in the creative process (i.e., whether the
"author" was God or Luke) or, therefore, the creative mode.
That is to say, placing a given work in one of Frye's fictional
modes is a critical statement of sorts about the work in question; but placing a given work in one of the following creative
modes is a critical statement not about the work itself but about
the criticism of the work. So, while the center of gravity of
creative modes, like the center of gravity of fictional modes,
has moved steadily down the list, that movement is not a
measure of the dominant narrative motif but of the dominant
critical motif. In order to apply Frye's statement to the creative
modes, one would have to modify it to read: "European *criticism*, during the last fifteen centuries, has steadily moved its
center of gravity down the list." And though the center of
gravity of creative modes has moved down the list in a roughly
chronological manner, it should be emphasized that these are
modes and do not strictly demarcate historical periods.

The five creative modes are these:[1]

(1) If the archive given to the artisan by the arché is a more
or less finished script, the creation is in the *transcendental*
mode. In this mode, the arché is often a divine being (the Muses,
for instance, or God). The function of the artisan is merely to
record what is "dictated" by the arché with no input of his own.
The artisan's function in the transcendental mode is analogous
to the function of a tape recorder or of a secretary taking dictation.

(2) If the archive given to the artisan by the arché is not a

script but an idea or plan, the creation is in the *ideal* mode. In this mode, the artisan does not "record" the archive, she "encodes" it; so that creation in the ideal mode is seen as very roughly analogous to translation of a work from one language to another.

(3) If the archive given to the artisan by the arché is a special power or ability, the creation is in the *formal* mode. Here the artisan is thought of on analogy with an alchemist, as one who is able, through a mysterious skill based on heightened sensibilities, to transform the base metals of ordinary experience in the natural world into golden art.

(4) If there is no "divine" arché outside the artisan, then the artisan has no special power, and the creation is in the *real* mode. The artisan in this mode is simply one of us.

(5) If the ore is itself the arché, then it is the ore that determines the shape of the artifact, and the artisan is essentially invisible or powerless. When this is so, the creation is in the *empirical* mode. The archive is the artifact, and the reader becomes more powerful than the artisan. In this last mode, the artisan is thought of on analogy with, say, Pheidippides, who dies upon delivering his message, or with the male spider that is devoured by the female after his task is done.

Frye says that, having distinguished fictional modes, one must be ready then to recombine them. "For while one mode constitutes the underlying tonality of a work of fiction, any or all of the other four may be simultaneously present" (50). In fact, it is through such modal counterpointing that "we may come to realize that the two essential facts about a work of art, that it is contemporary with its own time and that it is contemporary with ours, are not opposed but complementary facts" (51). Similarly, a work may be thought of as exemplifying more than one creative mode. However, the reason for the possibility of plural creative modes is different from the reason for the possibility of plural fictional modes. In the case of creative modes, since what is at issue is not the story in which the hero participates but the story of how the work originated, the dominant creative mode attributed to a work will depend as much on the critical theory or ideology of the reader as on the work itself. It is this "recombination" of creative modes that prevents our thinking of the generally downward trend of the "center of gravity" of the modes as a strict historical progression, for it means that regardless of the dominant mode in a given work or at a given point in time, other modes will still be present in varying degrees.

Frye's fictional modes also "help to explain something that might otherwise be a puzzling fact about modern literature. Irony descends from the real: it begins in realism and dispassionate observation. But as it does so, it moves steadily towards myth, and dim outlines of sacrificial rituals and dying gods begin to reappear in it. Our five modes evidently go around in a circle" (42). A similar claim might be made about the creative modes. Though there is more of the recombination mentioned above in the case of creative modes than there is in the case of fictional modes, it is still true that the transcendental mode leads to the ideal mode and so on until the empirical mode at last leads back into the transcendental mode; and a case can still be made for a roughly historical progression. The presence of recombination in such a degree, though, limits my claims about the progression of the modes to a strict claim only about their conceptual progression, and a necessarily looser, more general claim about their historical progression. I will consider one or two examples from each creative mode, and conclude with an example of the usefulness of the classification of modes, in which I will use the transition from the empirical to the transcendental mode to explain not, as in Frye, a puzzling fact about modern literature, but a puzzling fact about ancient literature instead.

The Transcendental Mode

This mode I call "transcendental" because the arché and archive alike are outside the realm of normal human experience. There are two primary archetypes for this mode, one from the Greeks and one from the Hebrews. The Greek archetype is the oracle. H. W. Parke defines an oracle as "a formal statement from a god, usually given in answer to an enquiry, or else the place where such an enquiry could be made" (1967, 9). The oracle provided a "method of ascertaining the will of the gods" in a culture that "possessed, generally speaking, no sacred books" (9). That method was for an enquirer (who might be a state, a ruler, or a private citizen) to ask of a god through the mediation of a priest, priestess, or prophet a question, frequently one concerning future events, that the enquirer himself was unable to answer. The god (arché), from his store of divine knowledge (ore), formulated an answer (archive) that he transmitted to a mediating agent (artisan) who relayed the message (now the artifact) in either verbal or written form to the enquirer.

There were several locations of oracles and also several kinds of oracles in the ancient world. The location of an oracle was, according to F. W. H. Myers, most often "some chasm or cleft in the ground, filled, perhaps, with mephitic vapours, or with the mist of a subterranean stream, or merely opening in its dark obscurity an inlet into the mysteries of the underworld" (1911, 10). Myers lists several other frequent locations: fetish-stones, posts for the observation of birds or lightning, groves, streams, and mountain summits. All, though, share one feature: They were regions that would have "seemed to bring the unseen close to man" (11). The location, then, facilitates the artisan's work of mediation; only in certain places is it possible for the divine archive to "cross over" into the world as a human artifact. A particularly vivid account of this is found in Diodorus Siculus's account of the origin of divination at Delphi, in which the holy site was discovered by a herdsman whose goats began to leap about whenever one of them looked down into the chasm. The herdsman himself was affected when he approached the chasm, and he began to prophesy; word of these prodigies spread, and an oracle was born.

The variety of the kinds of divination practiced in oracles was limited only by the animistic imagination of the ancients. There was ornithomancy, divination by the flight of birds; pyromancy, divination by fire; hieromancy, divination by the entrails of sacrificial animals; cleromancy, divination by lots; and many other kinds. In addition, there was the kind most often associated with the word "oracle," namely, "genuine *mantike*," which was "divination . . . directly inspired by a god and independent of any material signs" and which was "caused by possession, by the literal presence of the god in the soul of the prophet or prophetess" (Flacelière 1965, 20). Flacelière emphasizes the difference between divination by signs and inspired divination, but the two kinds are equally suited to their function as archetypal transcendental creation. The difference between divination by signs and inspired divination lies not in the creative mode, but in the nature of the artisan. In inspired divination, the artisan is the prophet or prophetess. In divination by signs, however, the artisan is not a human being; in ornithomancy, for example, the role of the artisan is fulfilled by the birds whose flight signals the god's answer.

This perhaps calls for explanation. Consider inspired divination. In some cases, the prophet or prophetess (the artisan) uttered or wrote the prophecy in the immediate presence of the enquirer, while in others (Delphi, for instance) the message might be put into hexameter verse by a third party. The third party, though, always acts *ex post facto*, after the prophecy (the artifact) has been delivered. The same is true of divination by signs. Certain activities (artifacts) of birds (artisans) had standard meanings and could be immediately understood by all observers, while for others the service of trained seers was employed; but the seers always acted as interpreters, not as participants in the creative process. The variety of types of oracles points to the paradoxical role of the artisan in the transcendental creative mode. That the artisan in transcendental creation may be a dream or a bird or the entrails of an ox as easily as it may be a human being attests to the unimportance of the artisan. The artisan is only a tool of the gods. However, that there is invariably an intermediary (artisan) of some sort attests to the artisan's importance. The artisan is a tool, but he or she (or it) is a tool *of the gods*. And the variety of types of oracles also helps to explain why divination without signs was *mantike*; why, in other words, the artisan was always mad or blind. The madness or blindness, in other respects a defect, was an aid to divination because it loosened one's connection to this world, and made one for that reason more suitable as a tool for the gods' use.

If one were concerned to establish the circular progression of dominant modes (given, as I attempt to show below, that the currently dominant mode is the empirical mode), or if one were concerned, more modestly, to show the persistence into the present time of the "oracular" archetype of the creative mode, two related examples would be available. The first is the popular "Ouija" board game, in which the planchette is supposed to convey the messages of spirits. Or, for an example of a literary work, one might point to James Merrill's recent epic poem,

The Changing Light at Sandover, the pretext for which is the communication of certain spirits through Ouija materials.

The Hebrew archetype for the transcendental creative mode is the production of the Ten Commandments, and the Bible gives two accounts of that production. In both accounts, the Israelites are camped near Mount Sinai, and in both accounts the Decalogue is given twice. Moses goes up on the mountain into the presence of the Lord, is given the law, spends forty days and forty nights, and returns only to find that the people have set up a golden image, which they are worshipping. Moses is upset, dashes the tablets to the ground, destroys the image, and chastises the people. He then returns to the mountain and receives the law once more on the two tables of stone he has hewn from the earth. But there is for our purposes an important difference between the two accounts. In Deuteronomy, the law is always written onto the tables by the finger of God (see 5:22, 9:8–12, 10:1–5); but in Exodus, the law in some passages is said to have been written by the finger of God (24:12–14, 31:18, 32:15), while in others it is said to have been written by Moses' hand (34:27–29).

Consider first the version in which Moses does the writing:

The Lord said to Moses, "Cut two tables of stone like the first; and I will write upon the tables the words that were on the first tables, which you broke. Be ready in the morning, and come up in the morning to Mount Sinai, and present yourself there to me on the top of the mountain. . . ." So Moses cut two tables of stone like the first; and he rose early in the morning and went up on Mount Sinai, as the Lord had commanded him, and took in his hand two tables of stone. And the Lord descended in the cloud and stood with him there, and proclaimed the name of the

Lord. The Lord passed before him and proclaimed, [etc.] . . . And the Lord said to Moses, "Write these words; in accordance with these words I have made a covenant with you and with Israel." And he was there with the Lord forty days and forty nights; he neither ate bread nor drank water. And he wrote upon the tables the words of the covenant, the ten commandments. (*Exodus* 34)

Here the process might be expressed in terms of our model of creation as follows. God's knowledge of what is just and good, and so on, is the ore; God himself is the arché; the Decalogue is the archive; Moses is the artisan; and the tables are the artifact. This version of the production of the Ten Commandments is an ideal example of the transcendental creative mode: The arché is a divine being; he gives the artisan a finished script as the archive; and the artisan simply records what is "dictated" by the arché with no input of his own.

But what of the other version, in which God himself writes on the tables of stone? Consider this part of Deuteronomy 10, in which Moses is speaking:

"At that time the Lord said to me, 'Hew two tables of stone like the first, and come up to me on the mountain, and make an ark of wood. And I will write on the tables the words that were on the first tables which you broke, and you shall put them in the ark.' So I made an ark of acacia wood, and hewed two tables of stone like the first, and went up the mountain with the two tables in my hand. And he wrote on the tables, as at the first writing, the ten commandments which the Lord had spoken to you on the mountain out of the midst of the fire on the day of the assembly; and the Lord gave them to me. Then I turned and came down from the mountain, and put the

tables in the ark which I had made; and there they are, as
the Lord commanded me."

This version agrees with the version above in everything except
who actually does the writing. Moses hews the tables, brings
them to God, and transmits them to the people. In fact, Moses
is still apparently considered essential in this version, just as
he is when he does the writing, for the people are still forbidden
by God and by their own fear to approach the mountain, and
Moses still asks (only seven verses after the passage just quoted),
"And now, Israel, what does the Lord your God require of you,
but . . . to keep the commandments and statutes of the Lord,
which *I* command you this day for your good?" (my emphasis).
Moses still performs essential tasks of mediation even when he
does not perform the "standard" artisan's mediating task of
writing. He now has the same paradoxical role the artisan has
in the oracular archetype of the transcendental mode: important but unimportant, indispensable but secondary. If the version in which Moses writes the law on the tables is *an ideal
example* of the transcendental creative mode, the version in
which God writes the law on the tables is *the ideal* of the
transcendental creative mode. The artisan is still a necessary
condition for the "crossover" of the archive into the human
world as an artifact: He must hew the stones and he must
deliver them to the people; no one else can come onto the
mountain "lest the Lord break out upon them." But he is "invisible" as regards the archive's becoming an artifact: The artifact,
because it has not been made impure by human imperfection,
is a perfect copy of the archive; it is true and flawless as nothing
made by a human could be. This is the purpose of the artisan
in the transcendental creative mode: He is to communicate the
archive with as little distortion as possible, and with no "input"
of his own.

The Gospel of John speaks of the delivery of the Ten Commandments as a typological prefiguring of redemption: "For the law was given through Moses; grace and truth came through Jesus Christ." But as has been shown, it also serves in its two versions as (1) the ideal and (2) an ideal example of an important conception of artistic creation; so that conjoining these two services, we may speak of the delivery of the Ten Commandments, like the Greek oracle, as an archetype of the transcendental creative mode.

As with the oracular archetype, there are examples to demonstrate the persistence into the present time of the biblical archetype of the transcendental creative mode and the circular progression of the creative modes. In fact, it would be possible to trace one history of the modes from transcendental to empirical in the history of biblical criticism, and in particular in the history of doctrines of inspiration. The recent resurgence of "fundamentalism" in evangelical denominations in the United States is one instance of the presence of the transcendental creative mode today. Harold Lindsell, for instance, claims to believe that biblical inerrancy is "the most important theological topic of this age" (1976, 13). He claims further that what makes the Bible inerrant is "the very nature of inspiration" (31). The Bible, in other words, owes all its authority to the manner in which it was created; had it been inspired in a different way (created in a different mode), it would not have the authority it now does. And the inspiration he speaks of fits perfectly into the pattern of transcendental creation: "The Bible was written by human and divine agencies; that is, it was the product of God and chosen men. The authors of Scripture [artisans] retained their own styles of writing and the Holy Spirit [arché], operating within this human context, so superintended the writing of the Word of God that the end product [the artifact] was God's [i.e., it faithfully reproduced the archive]" (31).

The Ideal Mode

The difference between the transcendental creative mode and the ideal creative mode is that in the transcendental mode the artisan is given a more or less finished script, which she simply records in an attempt to make the artifact a "word-for-word" reproduction of the archive; but in the ideal mode the artisan is given instead an idea or a plan (hence the name "ideal"), which she herself must put into words. One good example of the ideal mode is Anselm's *Proslogion,* or, more specifically, two stories describing its creation, one in its preface and the other in Eadmer's biography of Anselm.

The story Anselm tells in the preface to the *Proslogion* is in four main steps. First, after having written the *Monologion,* a tract composed of "a connected chain of many arguments" intended to show that God exists, that he is the supreme good, and so on, Anselm "began to wonder if perhaps it might not be possible to find [*inveniri*] one single argument [to prove that God exists, etc.] that for its proof required no other save itself" (1965, 105). Second, he became despondent over his lack of success, and "decided to put aside this idea altogether, lest by uselessly occupying my mind it might prevent other ideas with which I could make some progress." Third, the idea began to force itself on Anselm in spite of his unwillingness, until "one day when I was quite worn out with resisting its importunacy, there came to me, in the very conflict of my thoughts, what I had despaired of finding, so that I eagerly grasped the notion which in my distraction I had been rejecting." And fourth, Anselm wrote the *Proslogion* in order to preserve and publish "what had given me such joy to discover."

Eadmer's account is slightly fuller. In it, as in Anselm's own account, Anselm becomes dissatisfied with the *Monologion* and decides to "try to prove by one single and short argument the things which are believed and preached about God" (1972, 29). Also as in the preface, Anselm becomes despondent over his lack of success, but this time he is despondent for different reasons: "partly because thinking about it took away his desire for food, drink and sleep, and partly . . . because it disturbed the attention which he ought to have paid to matins and to Divine service at other times." In Eadmer's account, Anselm's reason for "[trying] to banish it from his mind" is that "he supposed that this line of thought was a temptation of the devil" (30). But still the thought pursued him, until "suddenly one night during matins the grace of God illuminated his heart, the whole matter became clear to his mind, and a great joy and exultation filled his inmost being." Anselm "immediately and ungrudgingly" wrote (*scripsit*) the idea on wax tablets. But the record of the idea was to have, according to Eadmer, a troubled youth. The first wax tablets were lost by the monk entrusted with their safekeeping. Anselm wrote another draft (*dictamen*). This second draft was broken. Anselm recovered the writing (*scripturam recuperat*) by piecing together the broken tablets, and ordered the draft copied (*tradi*) onto parchment. And finally, Anselm composed (*composuit*) the final version.

What is important for our purposes is what the two accounts share. In each account the idea is given. Anselm himself actively pursues it, but fails in his pursuit. It is not until he has forsaken the attempt that the idea forces itself on him; in one account its origin is not specified, and in the other it is said to have been given by God. Similarly, in each account the production of the document containing the idea seems to be wholly Anselm's responsibility, both in the decision whether or not to record the idea at all, and in the method chosen to put the idea into words. Thus in the preface, Anselm decides to record the idea only because he thinks it will give pleasure to anyone who might happen to read it, and when he writes it, he decides to deal with this question "as well as several others"

(103). In Eadmer's account, Anselm writes his idea because he thinks "others also would be glad to know [it]" (30); and the many trials endured by the versions are evidence that responsibility for composition was Anselm's, since after each mishap a different Latin word is used to describe the way in which Anselm "wrote" his idea. So, translating these two descriptions of the composition of the *Proslogion* into the terminology of the model, it may be said that the ore is something like God's knowledge of himself, and so on; God is the arché; the idea that forces itself on Anselm is the archive; Anselm is the artisan; and the *Proslogion* is the artifact.

If the scope of the discussion is expanded now from a single work to the mind-set of a historical period, one of the central projects of medieval philosophy, the attempt to demonstrate the essential agreement between faith and reason, presents itself in a new light. Special revelation had ceased, so for the medieval philosophers creation in the transcendental mode was, they knew, impossible for them. But it was still possible for them to reformulate the already given truths "in their own way," that is, in the ideal mode. If this is so, then even if one ignores claims like the one in Eadmer of God's unmediated activity in a writer's mind, certain phenomena like the desire (especially manifest in Anselm) to prove scriptural truths by reason alone without reference to Scripture can still be explained. The ideas were still given (whether through Scripture or the direct activity of God), but the words had to be found.

The Formal Mode

The change from the ideal mode to the formal mode is, like the change from the transcendental mode to the ideal mode, primarily a change in the nature of the archive, which produces secondary changes in the other elements of the model. In the ideal mode, the archive was an idea or plan given the artisan by the arché. In the formal mode, the archive is a special power or ability to create. This mode is called "formal" because "form, it should be remembered, is a word that has several meanings, some of which are contradictory. For instance, form has to do with the structure or outward appearance of something but it also has to do with its essence" (Strand 1982, 454). And in this mode the artisan is trans*formed* by the power or ability she receives; further, she is able in virtue of her gift to change the form (appearance and essence) of the ordinary things of common life. Wordsworth's "Preface" to the *Lyrical Ballads* is an instance of a work committed to the formal mode, and the transition from ideal to formal is evident in his discussion of the purpose of the poems as well as in his discussion of the role of the poet.

Wordsworth describes the principal object of the poems in *Lyrical Ballads* as having been "to choose incidents and situations from common life, and to relate or describe them, throughout, as far as was possible in a selection of language really used by men, and, at the same time, to throw over them a certain colouring of imagination, whereby ordinary things should be presented to the mind in an unusual aspect" (1932, 935). The poems, then, have their roots in common life and common language, not in the divine world of the transcendental and ideal creative modes. The subjects of the poems are accessible to all persons, rather than being given only to the artisan, as is the case in the transcendental and ideal modes. What makes the poems extraordinary is the special "colouring" cast over them by the poet's special imagination. It is this imagination, not the subjects of the poems, that only the artisan has. The result is "a selection of the real language of men in a state of vivid sensation" (934).

The poet himself differs only in degree, not in kind, from other men (939). He is a man "possessed of more than usual organic sensibility" (935). Wordsworth offers the following answer to the question "What is a poet?":

> He is a man speaking to men: a man, it is true, endowed
> with more lively sensibility, more enthusiasm and
> tenderness, who has a greater knowledge of human nature,
> and a more comprehensive soul, than are supposed to be
> common among mankind; a man pleased with his own
> passions and volitions, and who rejoices more than other
> men in the spirit of life that is in him; delighting to
> contemplate similar volitions and passions as manifested
> in the goings-on of the Universe, and habitually impelled
> to create them where he does not find them. To these
> qualities he has added a disposition to be affected more
> than other men by absent things as if they were present;
> an ability of conjuring up in himself passions, which are
> indeed far from being the same as those produced by real
> events, yet (especially in those parts of the general
> sympathy which are pleasing and delightful) do more
> nearly resemble the passions produced by real events, than
> anything which, from the motions of their own minds
> merely, other men are accustomed to feel in themselves:—
> whence, and from practice, he has acquired a greater
> readiness and power in expressing what he thinks and
> feels, and especially those thoughts and feelings which, by
> his own choice, or from the structure of his own mind,
> arise in him without immediate external excitement. (937)

All of this may be translated into the terms of the model of creation in the following way. The arché is no longer God or the gods, but is now Nature. And the ore, consequently, is changed from the divine knowledge or the like to natural experiences likely to be common to all humans. But the arché, Nature, still gives the artisan a special gift; only in the formal mode the gift is not that which is to become the artifact, but that which enables the artisan herself to produce the artifact. The archive is the poet's special endowment of sensibility, her "more comprehensive soul." In the formal mode, the artisan attains her most unambiguous honor; in none of the other modes does she have such stature.

The Real Mode

This mode is called "real" because the central part of the creative process, from arché to artisan, is embodied or reified in the artist. In the real mode, the artisan begins her descent from prominence. The arché is no longer divine, so the artisan no longer communes with the divine, receives divine gifts, or even has special powers bestowed on her by God or Nature. The artisan in the real mode is simply one of us. I will consider as an example of this mode Freud's comments concerning creation.

For Freud, artistic creation is only one of "various forms of activity" into which "psychical instinctual force" is converted (1959b, 75). Among the other forms into which it is converted are dreams and neurotic symptoms. There are two differences between works of art on the one hand and dreams and neurotic symptoms on the other. The first is that works of art, unlike dreams and symptoms, are calculated to gratify the same unconscious wishes in other people that they do in the artist himself. And the second is that works of art make use "of the perceptual pleasure of formal beauty as . . . an 'incitement-premium'." But there are more important similarities between works of art and dreams and symptoms. First, all three (artworks, dreams, and symptoms) are "imaginary gratifications of unconscious wishes," and second, all three "are in the nature of compromises" and "are forced to avoid any open conflict with the forces of repression" (1959a, 64–65). It is noteworthy that the similarities are similarities of origin, but that the differences are post-originary additions, so that for Freud the manner of creation of works of art is essentially the same as the manner of creation of dreams and symptoms.

Consider, then, Freud's description of the origin of dreams. In producing a dream, the mind makes use of its store of past experiences (primarily its childhood sexual experiences), the residues of the experiences of the day preceding the dream (primarily residues of unsatisfactorily completed experiences, or "unfinished business"), and, in some cases, internal or external stimuli during sleep. These, in the terminology of the model I am using here, are the ore. Two agencies have a hand in the production of the dream. The first agency produces the latent dream-thought(s), a wish or wishes, out of the ore. This agency is the arché, and the latent dream-thought is the archive. The second agency, however, distorts by an act of censorship the latent dream-thought from its original form, which is inadmissible to our waking thoughts, into a form (the manifest dream) that is admissible. The second agency is the artisan, and the manifest dream is the artifact. Freud gives us to infer that the only changes that need to be made to this account of dream creation to make it into an account of artistic creation are: (1) A work of art is unlikely to make use of stimuli during sleep; (2) the wish (or wishes) produced by the first agency is not a latent dream-thought, but the latent artwork; and (3) the second agency distorts the first agency's wish or wishes into a work of art rather than into a dream.

The important change that occurs in the movement from the previous modes to the real mode results primarily from the "fall" of the arché from a divine level (either a god or gods, or Nature) to a human level, and the consequent shift in the balance of authority to the artisan. In Freud, the arché has fallen to the level of the unconscious; and although the unconscious is for Freud the "true psychical reality," it is nonetheless the origin of all the traditionally "base" or "animal" features of human nature and is in that sense "sub-human." Where the artisan has previously been attempting to reproduce the archive accurately (or in the formal mode at least to be true to it), in Freud the artisan is struggling *against* the archive, trying to erase or distort it, trying to deprive it of its force. Art is no longer an attempt to bring down into the human world something originally or essentially divine; it has become an attempt (by sublimating the psychical instinctual forces) to elevate into the civilized human world something that originates in the uncivilized part of man. The artisan need not be seen as struggling against the arché for creation to be in the real mode. The archive might be thought of as a gift from the unconscious, say, or as something that "just came to me." Freud is useful as an example, though, because thinking of the artisan as struggling against the arché "within" him is a possibility in the real mode, but not, as will soon be clear, in the empirical mode.

The Empirical Mode

In the empirical mode the ore takes over the role of the arché; the mode is called "empirical" because, unlike the transcendental mode, the dominant or originary part of the creative process is something that is an integral part of human experience. The ore determines the shape and the possibilities of the archive. But in this mode the ore does more than that. It also determines the shape and the possibilities of the artifact. The artisan is essentially powerless, invisible. This mode is exemplified by much of the recent criticism classed as "structuralist."

Consider the first three pages of an influential book by Jonathan Culler on structuralism. There, attempting to establish

104

the important role linguistics has played and continues to play in the development of structuralism, Culler says: "Linguistics is not simply a stimulus and source of inspiration but a methodological model which unifies the otherwise diverse projects of structuralists" (1975, 4). And the usefulness of linguistics as a stimulus and a model is based, he says, "on two fundamental insights: first, that social and cultural phenomena are not simply material objects or events but objects or events with meaning, and hence signs; and second, that they do not have essences but are defined by a network of relations, both internal and external." Thus "if human actions or productions have a meaning there must be an underlying system of distinctions and conventions which makes this meaning possible." The upshot of the two insights is this:

> When one takes as object of study not physical phenomena, but artefacts or events with meaning, the defining qualities of the phenomena become the features which distinguish them one from another and enable them to bear meaning within the symbolic system from which they derive. The object is itself structured and is defined by its place in the structure of the system, whence the tendency to speak of 'structuralism'. (5)

To translate this now into the terminology of the model: "The system" is the ore. It is the "material" from which the artifact arises. But the ore in this mode has powers not attributed to it in the other modes. The symbolic system has usurped the role of the arché, for it is the origin of the archive; it is that which determines the possibilities and limits of the artisan; it is the artisan's only resource. And its power does not stop there. It shapes the artifact as well, rendering the artisan essentially invisible. In the real mode, the possibilities of the artisan are circumscribed, to be sure. It is given certain material from the ore by the arché, and all it can do is to modify that material as far as possible to suit its intentions. But in the empirical mode the possibilities of the artisan are even more narrowly circumscribed. For here the system of conventions (ore and arché) not only gives the artisan his material (the archive), but it also determines the possibilities and the meanings of his actions; he cannot, in other words, struggle against the arché as can the artisan in the real mode, for he is himself a product of, and he operates within, the system that is the ore and arché. And since the artifact not only arises from but also takes its place within the symbolic system, it is no longer structured by a poet (an artisan) but, to requote Culler, "by its place in the structure of the system."

The important difference between the example given for the real mode and that given for the empirical mode is that for Freud the unconscious (the arché) is individual and is within the human being. But for the structuralists, language is an *inter*personal, *im*personal system that is in a very important sense outside the human being. For Freud, the functions of the arché and the artisan both can be located within the individual creating the work; but for the structuralists, only the function of the artisan can be spoken of as located within the individual. For Freud, artistic creation is the result of humans *qua* humans; but for the structuralists, artistic creation is the result of humans *qua* instruments of systems of signification.

The examples of the five creative modes are, of course, only examples; as such, each example only typifies but does not define or delimit the mode it represents. Further, it is important to observe that the modes are not mutually exclusive. Vestiges of more than one mode may be present in a single work or view of a work. For instance, Donald Justice describes his method of writing poetry in this way: "I write or try to write as if convinced that, prior to my attempt, there existed a true text, a sort of Platonic script, which I had been elected to transcribe or record" (1984, 138). The "as if" indicates that Justice holds a view best classified in the real mode, but the hypothetical Platonic scripts are obvious traces of the transcendental mode. The modes, then, are best thought of, not on analogy with a pie cut neatly into five slices, but on analogy with colors: The bounds within the spectrum are not rigid, and colors can be mixed.

The modes disclose an important fact about the model: The terms denote not fixed entities but functions, not constants but variables. The arché, for instance, in the transcendental mode is often a divinity, as is the case with claims of strict verbal inspiration for the Bible, where the arché is the Christian God; in the real mode, however, the arché is not even thought of as an individual apart from the artisan, but is located within the artisan, so that the artisan, if asked about the origin of her work, might say something like, "The idea just came to me." The terms of the model, then, are parameters, whose value varies with each specific application.

The artisan in the five creative modes is on a sort of "wheel of fortune." In the transcendental mode, she is important only as a "channel" through which the work flows; she contributes nothing of her own (nothing "original") to the work. In the ideal mode, the artisan's role is more important. She is given an idea, but she is responsible for the formulation of the idea. The artisan reaches her apotheosis in the formal mode, where she is given a talent that enables her to turn dross into gold, chaff into wheat. In the real mode, the artisan returns to the level of the ordinary, the merely human. And in the empirical mode, the artisan is once more essentially invisible; she is returned to the status of merely a messenger or a channel through which the archive becomes the artifact. Now it is easy to see why the path of the modes is circular, and why a *wheel* of fortune is therefore appropriate as a metaphor. For it is only a short step from a mode in which the words that constitute a system of signs, acting as arché and having power over the artisan, control the creation of the artifact, to a mode in which the Word, acting as arché and having power over the artisan, controls the creation of the artifact.

The progression from the empirical mode to the transcendental mode is not only plausible as a logical progression, though. A case can be made for its having occurred already as a historical progression as well. My examples of the transcendental mode above were the Greek oracle and the delivery of the Ten Commandments. But our information about those is (in the former case) largely or (in the latter case) wholly based on written documents from literate cultures. What of earlier times, like the transition from an illiterate to a literate society? At least one record of such a transition exists: the story of Bellerophontes in the *Iliad*. As the illiterate bard tells us, King Proitos, angry over his wife's accusation that Bellerophontes had tried to seduce her, tries to have him killed. In Lattimore's translation, "He shrank from killing him, since his heart was awed by such action, / but sent him away to Lykia, and handed him murderous symbols, / which he inscribed on a folding tablet, enough to destroy life, / and told him to show it to his wife's father, that he might perish" (Homer 1961, Bk. 6, ll. 167–70, p. 157).

What is striking about the Bellerophontes story is the degree to which Proitos, supposedly the one who wants to murder Bellerophontes, is a pawn of other forces in the attempted murder. Proitos was "seized by anger" on hearing his wife's words, he himself shrank from killing Bellerophontes, and instead gave him the deadly signs that were themselves sufficient to kill, so that Bellerophontes might be killed. Even taking into account the obvious limitation of this example, namely, that unlike modern examples of the empirical mode the composer of this passage, being illiterate, would not be able to think of the writing of signs as the creation of a work of art, it is still strikingly similar to the modern structuralist theory I have described as exemplary of the empirical mode, at least in the power it attributes to language, and in particular to writing, at the expense of the writer, who is seen as less powerful than the writing itself. And if, as H. L. Lorimer writes, "the air of magic and mystery with which the poet invests [writing] is still in the eighth century [B.C.] appropriate, whereas in the seventh it would have been absurd" (1950, 474), it has become appropriate once more in the twentieth century A.D., just as the fear of God, appropriate for the ignorant indigene but absurd for the "religious" masses, may become appropriate again for the studied theologian.

I promised above to offer an explanation of a puzzling fact about ancient literature, and the observation of the ease with which one might move from the empirical creative mode to the transcendental creative mode, combined with the observation that a newly literate culture like that of the ancient Greeks might begin with a conception of literary creation in the empirical mode, makes possible that explanation. The fact that I will attempt to explain is Plato's criticism of poetry, which is puzzling because, in Gadamer's words, "probably nowhere else has a philosopher denied the value of art so completely and so sharply contested its claim—which seems so self-evident to us—to reveal the deepest and most inaccessible truths" (1980, 39). Plato's position concerning poetry is, to borrow (and sully) Horace's later turn of phrase, that it is able to delight but not to teach.[2] His criticism is based on two accusations: (1) that poetry does not represent reality accurately, and (2) that poetry cannot defend itself against misinterpretation.

The first charge receives its most famous formulation in Book 10 of the *Republic*. There Plato argues that poetry is "three removes from nature" (1961, 597e): The god produces one type of couch; the carpenter produces a second type of couch, which is an imitation of the first type; and the artist (painter or poet) produces a third type, which is an imitation of the second type. Plato's image for craftsman and artist alike is a mirror. The difference between the two is that the craftsman mirrors reality, while the artist mirrors appearance. Here is an instance that Richard Rorty well could have cited as an example of his thesis that "philosophy's central concern is to be a general theory of representation" (1980, 3) and that "the picture which holds traditional philosophy captive is that of the mind as a great mirror, containing various representations" (12).[3] What I want to suggest is that Plato's argument can be profitably viewed in terms of the creative modes. The procedure of the craftsman seems most closely to resemble the transcendental mode. The craftsman himself performs the role of the artisan; and if we take the mirror image seriously, his function is simply to record or re-present the real couch (the archive), which was itself made (given) by the god (arché). But the painter and the poet fit better into the empirical mode. As I have suggested above, the role of the artisan is similar in the transcendental and empirical modes at least in this sense: In the former, he attempts to (or is obliged to) re-present the archive as accurately as possible with little or no active input of his own, while in the latter, the artisan is only *able* to re-present the archive, and is capable of very little active input of his own. The archive (ultimately the ore) in the empirical mode determines the possibilities of the artifact, and this is exactly what happens in the artist's mirroring of appearance. So, regarding the first of Plato's two main criticisms of poetry, two observations might be made: first, the image of the "mirror of nature," which, as Rorty points out, becomes a powerful force in philosophy after Locke and Descartes, appears to be a remnant of the transcendental creative mode; and second, Plato's accusation that poetry fails to represent reality accurately is based on the view that poetry results from the empirical creative mode.

The second distinct accusation against poetry is that it cannot defend itself. This charge is leveled at writing, so written poetry at least is obviously implicated. As with the accusation that poetry does not accurately represent reality, the comparison is with painting:

> That's the strange thing about writing, which makes it truly analogous to painting. The painter's products stand before us as though they were alive, but if you question them, they maintain a most majestic silence. It is the same with written words; they seem to talk to you as though they were intelligent, but if you ask them anything about what they say, from a desire to be instructed, they go on telling you just the same thing forever. And once a thing is put in writing, the composition, whatever it may be, drifts all over the place, getting into the hands not only of those who understand it, but equally of those who have no business with it; it doesn't know how to address the right people, and not address the wrong. And when it is ill-treated and unfairly abused it always needs its parent to come to its help, being unable to defend itself. (*Phaedrus*, 275d–e)

This accusation might be taken as implicating not texts but readers; as complaining not about the nature of writing but about the lack of sound criticism. But there is a more satisfying reading, one that makes sense of this passage and also shows its relation to the first accusation. In the *Ion* (at 533e ff.), Socrates compares the "chain of inspiration" from Muse to audience to a string of iron rings connected to a magnet. The poet is the first ring; Ion, the rhapsode, is the middle ring; and the spectator is the last ring. The god is the magnet. Socrates goes on in the course of the dialogue to argue that the force from the magnet is imperfectly transmitted to the final ring. His conclusion bears on the passage from the *Phaedrus* above, for the problem with oral poetry in the *Ion* is that the spectator is imperfectly connected with the deity; and the problem with written poetry in the *Phaedrus* is likewise that the reader is imperfectly connected with reality, since the writing may be misconstrued. If the writing were adequate as a representation of reality, if it were perfectly transparent, it wouldn't *need* to defend itself, any more than the carpenter's couch needs to defend itself.

The two accusations isolated above, then, may be seen as correlates of the two meanings of the word *mimesis* that Havelock extracts from Plato's works. *Mimesis* is, in one sense, "the name of the active personal identification by which the audience sympathizes with the performance" (Havelock 1963, 26). Poetry, in this sense of *mimesis*, is able to delight because it is a successful instantiation of the empirical mode; it delights because the power of the text does not stay in the artisan's hands but is passed to the reader. But *mimesis* is also "the word *par excellence* for the over-all linguistic medium of the poet and his peculiar power through the use of this medium . . . to render an account of reality" (25); it is, in other words, "the total act of poetic representation" (26). In this sense of *mimesis*, poetry is unable to teach because it is not a transparent representation of reality, and is therefore in need of a defense against misinterpretation that it is unable to give itself. The conclusion I draw is that one way of explaining Plato's criticism of poetry is in terms of the creative modes, as follows. Plato holds a view that is best seen as a transition between the empirical and transcendental creative modes. For him, the poet (the artisan) is always a mirror, a *mimetes*, with the relatively passive role that is a feature shared by the transcendental and empirical modes. Poetry is able to delight because it can represent logos or appearance, and is therefore a successful instantiation of the empirical mode. But poetry cannot teach because it is unable to represent faithfully the Logos or reality, and is therefore unsuccessful as an instantiation of the transcendental mode.

Although there have been many studies of creative individuals and many attempts to account for creativity in psychological or philosophical terms, there have been to my knowledge no historical overviews of the theories themselves. The absence of such overviews has gone unnoticed perhaps because they are no more necessary to a creative artist than is, say, Kuhn's *The Structure of Scientific Revolutions* to a practicing physicist. Yet, just as Kuhn's book, whether its claims are right or wrong, is important to anyone who wishes to understand the nature of scientific theories and their impact on society, so an overview of ideas of creation is important to anyone who wishes to understand creative works and society's reaction to them. Such a historical overview, even though provisional, identifies a conceptual pattern in the transformations of the notion of creativity in our culture and is a necessary step toward understanding the author.

CHAPTER 6

Creative Dynamics

I distinguished earlier between a psychological concern and a technical concern in the study of artistic creation, and announced my intention to focus primarily on the technical concern. I proposed a way of looking at the creative process, beginning with five terms, using them as a heuristic device, and arriving at five modes of creation after the manner of Northrop Frye's fictional modes. These five creative modes provide a way of grouping the stories that can be told about how a work has come to be. They offer, that is, a provisional means of classification. But the explanatory power of the modes is limited primarily to this kind of "placing" or "comparison" and to cases like that of Plato in which a doctrine or idea in a work is based on a particular view of creation.

The creative modes are valuable, then, for noting certain similarities. But every creative act is unique: The way in which the Bible came to be is different from the way in which Wittgenstein's "Blue Book" and "Brown Book" came to be, and the way in which *Paradise Lost* came to be is different from the way in which Dickinson's "This is my letter to the world" came to be. So it is that, in addition to accounting for the similarities between creative acts, there is also a need to account for the differences. If the creative modes may be thought of as a rudimentary, provisional grammar of sorts, then what is needed is a creative syntax. This chapter will attempt to provide at least the beginnings of such a syntax, under the name of creative dynamics. I will identify certain forces that constitute differences between the creative histories of texts, giving an example in each case of a work in which that force is active, and show how these forces complicate the relations between the ore, arché, archive, artisan, and artifact. I will conclude with a consideration of the creative history of a single work, showing how the activity of these forces undermines the traditional assumption that the author of a work is a single historical individual.

The metaphor for artistic creation most obviously missing from the previous chapter is the metaphor of human procreation, in which the arché is thought of as impregnating the artisan with the archive. As one might expect, this metaphor has had a long history and persisting influence. It has manifested itself in ways as subtle as Thomas Thorpe's dedication of Shakespeare's sonnets to "the Only Begetter of These Insuing Sonnets," implying that Mr. W. H. as the arché impregnates the poet with the inspiration from which the poems were born, and in ways as direct as these statements by Carl Jung:

It is obvious enough that psychology, being the study of psychic processes, can be brought to bear upon the study of literature, for the human psyche is the womb of all the sciences and arts. (1933, 152)

It makes no difference whether the poet knows that his work is begotten, grows and matures with him, or whether he supposes that by taking thought he produces it out of the void. His opinion of the matter does not change the fact that his own work outgrows him as a child its mother. The creative process has feminine quality, and the creative work arises from unconscious depths—we might say, from the realm of the mothers. (170)

In most cases, the use of procreation as a metaphor for artistic creation has its basis in the ancient notion, itself a metaphor, that the father contributes the seed and the mother the soil (that is, that the father is the active contributor of all the essential materials, and the mother is the passive receptor) rather than the modern notion that the male contributes one part of the necessary material, the sperm, and the mother, in addition to being the "soil," contributes the other half of the necessary material, the egg. Frye, for instance, relies on the active/passive connotations of the ancient view in making a distinction between literature and "discursive verbal structures" based on whether the poet is thought of as father or mother, active or passive.

As long as the father of a poem is assumed to be the poet himself, we have once again failed to distinguish literature from discursive verbal structures. The discursive writer writes as an act of conscious will, and that conscious will, along with the symbolic system he employs for it, is set over against the body of things he is describing. But the poet, who writes creatively rather than deliberately, is not the father of his poem; he is at best a midwife, or, more accurately still, the womb of Mother Nature herself: her privates he, so to speak. (1957, 98)

The poet as father contributes conscious material and produces discursive verbal structures; the poet as mother receives unconscious material and bears literature.[1]

The acts relevant to the creation of another human being, as a glance at any popular sex manual or a trip to an adult bookstore will disclose, are infinite in variety. Each birth, like each work of art, has a unique history. But certain differences between procreative histories have consequences for the child's future, while others do not. For example, whether the mother and father engaged in intercourse in a Holiday Inn or a Chevy is likely to be indifferent as regards the child's future; the same is true of whether the intercourse took place in the afternoon or at midnight, and whether it took place after five minutes or an hour of foreplay. On the other hand, whether or not the mother and father were married to each other at the time of intercourse is likely to be very important to the child's future; the same is true of whether the mother was fifteen or thirty years old at the time, and perhaps even whether a condom failed during intercourse.

What is true of the procreative histories of children is also true of the creative histories of literary works. Certain of the differences that make a creative history unique are more relevant to the meaning or the interpretation of a work than are others. Whether, for example, William Carlos Williams had his stethoscope around his neck or in the pocket of his lab coat at the time he composed "Between Walls" is irrelevant to the interpretation of the poem. Or, for a more interesting case, consider this description of a creative technique used briefly by Donald Justice:

> I was interested in finding a further means of keeping myself distant. I thought it would be interesting to simulate a small computer without actually using one, and so I wrote words onto a great number of note cards, words which I had taken from passages of poems I admired. My own taste, in other words, was involved in the preparations, so that I might think of whatever result was to

come as mine, somewhat mine. . . . I divided the word
cards up into three groups, nouns, verbs, and adjectives,
from which I thought I could generate any other parts of
speech necessary to deal with the sentences. I then . . .
dealt myself a sentence, you might say. (1984, 55–56)[2]

It is true that there is a sense in which this creative technique
made a lasting difference to the poems: Presumably, the poems
that were written in this way would not have been created had
it not been for Justice's use of the technique. But the same could
be said of the baby born from intercourse in a Holiday Inn: If
the parents' reservation had been canceled and they had been
forced to stay in the airport overnight, they might not have
engaged in the act that resulted in the child. But that the motel
they did stay in was a Holiday Inn (instead of, say, a Howard
Johnson's) is likely to have little impact on the child's future,
and it could be argued that the fact that Justice made up cards
to help select the words of a poem (instead of choosing them
without the use of this "artificial" method) has little or no
impact on the meaning of the poem.

But there are differences in the creative histories of artworks
that are more relevant to the work's later history than those
just mentioned, and it is these more relevant differences that
will occupy the rest of this chapter. I will identify two kinds
of relevant differences, which I will call "displacement" and
"multiplication." Displacement will be further subdivided into
accidental displacement, limited displacement, and systematic
displacement. Multiplication will be further subdivided into
simple multiplication and complex multiplication. I will conclude with an analysis of a complicated case of authorship in
which several of these types of difference are operative.

Displacement

In displacement another distinct step is added to the creative process, in addition to the "typical" procedure of the arché using the ore and giving the archive to the artisan, who in turn produces the artifact.[3] The artisan and artifact from the original creation are displaced, and become in effect the arché and archive, respectively, of the "secondary" creation. An artifact, in other words, is modified after its initial creation by the action of a second artisan.

As noted above, the creative modes disclose about the model the important fact that the terms denote parameters, not fixed entities. Displacement discloses a second important fact about the model, a fact that is roughly the converse of the first. A specific item (an individual human, a book, etc.) may fulfill more than one function. The examples given under the descriptions of the three major kinds of displacement will illustrate this fact.

Accidental Displacement

Accidental displacement occurs during the reproduction of a work. As a work is passed from scribe to scribe or as it goes through the stages of book production, there is the possibility of error. Hence the name *accidental* displacement: The task of the scribe or the book producer is to reproduce the manuscript without change, so any change introduced during the process of reproduction should be accidental. Accidental displacement thus may be thought of as a variant of the transcendental creative mode: The original artisan, now functioning as the secondary arché, gives the artifact, now functioning as the secondary archive, to the scribe or printer, who functions as the secondary artisan and tries to reproduce the secondary archive with no input of his own. If the scribe or printer does his job correctly, the artifact produced by the scribe or printer will be word for word the same as the artifact produced by the original artisan. Under ideal circumstances, of course, this kind of displacement should be no more important than Donald Justice's use of cards to write a poem. But in fact this ideal is not always attained, and accidental displacement becomes important when changes do occur or when it is not known whether changes have or have not occurred.

The most obvious choice for an example of accidental displacement would be an ancient or medieval manuscript of which we have only a copy or copies. But accidental displacement of the sort that influences the shape of a work is not limited to archaic works. Consider, for example, the recent complete edition of Charles Olson's *The Maximus Poems*, edited by George F. Butterick. This edition collects in one volume the three earlier volumes of *Maximus Poems*. Even though the text was photographically reproduced from those earlier volumes, the editor still found it necessary to make corrections and account for numerous discrepancies. Butterick writes:

> It was imperative to go back to the original manuscripts to make sure an apparent or suspected error was in fact that, and to pinpoint the source of each mistake, so that it could be corrected, by tracing the publishing history of each poem backward from the original volume to any earlier separate volumes, to magazine or similar appearances, to manuscripts sent editors, and to original manuscripts surviving among the poet's papers at the University of Connecticut Library.
>
> The surprising discovery was the extent of error: of the seventy-seven poems first published during the poet's lifetime in magazines, anthologies, or as broadsides, only fourteen appear exactly as in the later published volumes

> or the original manuscripts. . . . The immediate problem in
> all cases was to determine which, if any, changes were
> authorized, which errors. (1983, 637–38)

And the editor points out that not all of the discrepancies were
minor ones. "Some," he says, "not only distort the meaning
but render quite the opposite of the poet's intention." For example, in one edition there is mentioned "a sentimental, anthropo-
morphizing 'humanness' that neither the poet's father 'nor I,
as workers, / are *infuriated* with' " (italics added) instead of
" '*infatuated*' with," as in another edition (638).

Accidental displacement is of all types of displacement the
easiest to deal with in at least this sense: The task facing the
editor (or reader) is least problematic here. To claim that the
task of interpretation as a whole is to reconstruct the author's
intention or to discern in the work the meaning the author
intended it to have is at best controversial. But the case is
different if instead of the whole of interpretation one limits
oneself to only accidental displacement: In that case, even the
most ardent advocate of critical pluralism will likely agree that
the task at hand is to reconstruct, insofar as it is possible,
the author's intended words, even though agreement on those
words will not lead to agreement about what they mean. Distinguishing accidental displacement from other kinds of displacement and other possible means of distortion in works allows
us to distinguish between an author's intended words and her
intended meaning, and makes it possible to justify the widely
held belief that the reconstruction of an author's intended
words where possible is important, but that the reconstruction
of her intended meaning where possible is less important.

Limited Displacement
By limited displacement I mean the translation or adaptation
of a work, usually into another language.[4] I refer to it as *limited*

displacement because, although the modification introduced
(the change into another language) is purposeful, that modification is limited by the text being translated. If accidental displacement may be thought of as a variant of the transcendental
creative mode, then limited displacement is perhaps best
thought of as a variant of the ideal creative mode. The secondary
artisan is given a script, to be sure, so that at first glance there
is a resemblance to the transcendental mode. But her task is
not to reproduce the words as a scribe recopying a manuscript
or a secretary taking dictation might do; her task is to capture,
insofar as it is possible, the "content" of the original artifact.
What the secondary artisan is really given, on a practical level,
is not a script to be reproduced but an idea or plan or content
to be reformulated.

Limited displacement is more obviously a significant difference than is accidental displacement because the content of a
work in one language can never be precisely reformulated in
another language, so that the ideal is not even attainable in
theory, much less in practice. Saussure has given a theoretical
foundation to what translators have known all along: that a
word in one language has no precise correlate in any other
language. Language is not, according to Saussure, a simple naming process in which a signifier is attached to a pre-existing,
fixed concept. If it were so, translation would be a mechanical
process of exchanging the word for a given concept in one
language for the word attached to the same concept in another
language. But Saussure argues that the content of a word "is
fixed only by the concurrence of everything that exists outside
it. Being part of a system, it is endowed not only with a signification but also and especially with a value, and this is something quite different" (1966, 115). Saussure's first example is
this: "Modern French *mouton* can have the same signification
as English *sheep* but not the same value, and this for several

reasons, particularly because in speaking of a piece of meat ready to be served on the table, English uses *mutton* and not *sheep*. The difference in value between *sheep* and *mouton* is due to the fact that *sheep* has beside it a second term while the French word does not" (115–16).

So theoretical linguistics has articulated why it is that no literary work can hope to be reproduced accurately in a language other than its own. But if Wallace Stevens is correct, there is reason to think that poetry is an acute case. Consider his words: "Above everything else, poetry is words; and . . . words, above everything else, are, in poetry, sounds. . . . A poet's words are of things that do not exist without the words" (1981, 32). The consequence of these words for a translator who took them to heart would be that, since the nature of translation is to replace words with other words, the sound of which will be different, translation is no longer a reformulation of content with a certain amount of inevitable loss, but a complete destruction of content (the sound of the words) and the replacement of that content with other content. And even if one does not follow Stevens that far, it still seems to be the case that sound (not merely sound *qua* conjoined with a concept as in any linguistic sign, but sound *qua* sound) is an integral element of poetry, and an element that no translator could hope to reproduce.

Paul Valéry argues for a conclusion much like Stevens's: "If sound and sense (or form and content) can easily be dissociated, the poem *decomposes*," from which it follows that "the 'ideas' which figure in a work of poetry do not play the same role, and are not *the same kind of currency* at all, as the 'ideas' in prose" (1971, 91). Valèry says that his answer to the question of what he "wanted to say" in a given poem is "that I did not *want to say*, but *wanted to do*, and that it was the intention of *doing* which *wanted* what I *said*" (87). Of his poem "Le Cimetière Marin" he says, "this intention was originally no more than a rhythmic pattern, empty, or rather filled with meaningless syllables, which came to obsess me for a time" (87). The basic pattern was stanzas of six decasyllabic lines. But the rhythmic pattern, the sound of the words, can no more be reproduced in English than can the conceptual value of the words. Comparing even the first two lines of the translations of Graham Dustan Martin and John Finlay, one notices that Martin's translation does not reproduce the decasyllabic lines Valéry says are so important to the original. Finlay's translation manages that, but even Finlay's translation, despite its extraordinary attentiveness to sound, cannot reproduce, for instance, the rhyme.

> Valéry:
> Ce toit tranquille, où marchent des colombes,
> Entre les pins palpite, entre les tombes;
>
> Martin:
> This peaceful roof where doves are walking
> Pulses between the tombs, between the pines;
>
> Finlay:
> This tranquil vault, assuming files of doves,
> Is quivering between the pines and tombs.

Limited displacement, then, is in a sense a more severe form of displacement than accidental displacement, because it always results in alteration of the original, and that alteration is inevitably significant, while accidental displacement does not always result in alteration of the content of the original, and its alterations are usually less imposing than those made by limited displacement. The original and both translations of Valéry's poem have doves, but because of limited displacement the doves in each version are of a different species and have a different cry.

Systematic Displacement

The third type of displacement, systematic displacement, is potentially the most severe. In this type, the secondary artisan uses the original artifact in a way that serves her own ends. This is a form of displacement whether or not any resulting distortion of the artifact is intentional on the part of the secondary artisan. If accidental displacement is to be thought of as a variant of the transcendental creative mode and limited displacement is to be thought of as a variant of the ideal creative mode, then systematic displacement is perhaps best thought of on analogy with a cross between the transcendental and real modes. It shares with the transcendental mode the important feature that a script (the artifact) comes to the secondary artisan from outside herself. That script, though, is not from a divinity but from another human; it is a work of art. And as a result, systematic displacement shares with the real mode this feature: that the secondary artisan need not reproduce the original artifact faithfully. This is the sort of displacement that inevitably happens in criticism (and that has been happening during the course of this chapter), but a particularly vivid example is to be found in Aristotle's reproduction of the work of the Presocratic philosophers.

Harold Cherniss, in his important book *Aristotle's Criticism of Presocratic Philosophy*, argues that, though Aristotle surely had the books of the Presocratics in their complete form and though he was close to them in time, yet "nearer in time does not mean nearer in spirit," and according to Cherniss, "it can be shown that Aristotle was so consumed with the ideology of Platonism and the new concepts he had himself discovered or developed that it was impossible for him to imagine a time when thinking men did not see the problems of philosophy in the same terms as did he" (1935, x). If Cherniss is right, Aristotle's attitude is of a type not infrequent among critics, but it assumes a tremendous importance because in the case of the Presocratics there are precious few touchstones from sources other than Aristotle or one of his followers against which one seeking an "objective view" might test Aristotle's testimony. To test the statements of a critic (or, in other words, to nullify the possible distortion brought about by systematic displacement), one can normally return to the work in question; but with the Presocratics, there is no "pure" work to which one could return.

Cherniss argues that there are ways around this limitation, so that it still can be shown that Aristotle is not an objective commentator. For example: "We know that certain concepts and theories were introduced by Aristotle and others by Plato. If a Presocratic theory is presented in a way which involves such a notion, there is clearly something wrong with such a statement" (xi). The doxographical collections of Aristotle's reports of the Presocratics (Cherniss cites Emminger and Diels) "create," he says, "the false impression that Aristotle was interested in preserving the doctrines of the Presocratics for their own sake" (xi). But in fact, according to Cherniss, when one consults the context in which Aristotle's reports appear, one discovers that these reports "do not stand alone; they form an integral part of some argument which is meant to establish a positive doctrine of Aristotle's system, and the reports and interpretations vary with the doctrine that is being established" (xii). Cherniss says:

The conclusion is that Aristotle is not, in any of the works we have, attempting to give an historical account of earlier philosophy. He is using these theories as interlocutors in the artificial debates which he sets up to lead "inevitably" to his own solutions, for it is strikingly significant that these writings of his form one long series of dialogues in which one theory is set against another in such a manner that each may bring to light the other's difficulties which are then resolved by a reconciliation: this reconciliation is Aristotle's system. . . . Aristotle's belief that all previous theories were stammering attempts to express his own aids him in interpreting those theories out of all resemblance to their original form. (xii)

But if systematic displacement is potentially the most severe, and if Aristotle's use of the Presocratics is a case severe enough that the theories of the Presocratics have been distorted by Aristotle "out of all resemblance to their original form," there is at least this ray of hope: Since systematic displacement is distortion for a purpose, the direction to be taken by one hoping to nullify its effects is clear. She must attempt to remove the sediment of the secondary artisan's purpose. And this is just the method Cherniss settles on: One may hope, he says, to discover the reason for the variations in the reports, "and once the reason is so established there is a good chance with the aid of our other criteria of *stripping off the Aristotelian form* or at least of establishing in what direction the statement is likely to have deviated from the original meaning of the theory reported" (xiii; my emphasis). This is a method that must be applied tentatively, and whose results are sure to be qualified, but it is the only one available.

Multiplication

Displacement produces a "two-stage" effect, in which the artisan and artifact of the primary creation act as the arché and archive of the secondary creation. Multiplication, though, might or might not result in a two-stage effect. In multiplication, more than one item or individual share in the performance of a single function in the creative process. In other words, the role of the artisan, for example, may be performed by more than one individual. There are two main types of multiplication: simple and complex.

Simple Multiplication

In simple multiplication, there is a set of variant items instead of a single item functioning as artifact. In other words, more than one artifact has been produced. It is important to distinguish simple multiplication from accidental displacement. In accidental displacement, what is important is the movement from "original" to "copy" (from manuscript to book, for example), and not the fact that certain kinds of reproduction, like book publishing, are able to produce any number of identical copies. In accidental displacement, there may be only one copy, or there may be a million copies, all identical; what matters is the difference(s) between the original artifact and the secondary artifact. In simple multiplication, though, the transition from original to copy is not the central issue. More than one of the artifacts may be "an original," or it may be impossible to tell which artifact is an original and which a copy. What is important in simple multiplication is the difference(s) between the artifacts themselves.[5]

A well-known example of simple multiplication is Keats's "Ode on a Grecian Urn." No autograph manuscript version of the poem survives, but the last two lines of the several published versions vary in such a way that the choice of a version of the last lines significantly affects the interpretation of the poem. Among the different versions of the last lines are these:

> When old age shall this generation waste,
>   Thou shalt remain, in midst of other woe
> Than ours, a friend to man, to whom thou say'st,

'Beauty is truth, truth beauty,—that is all
  Ye know on earth, and all ye need to know.'

'Beauty is truth,—Truth Beauty,—that is all
  Ye know on Earth, and all ye need to know.

Beauty is Truth, Truth Beauty.—That is all
  Ye know on Earth, and all ye need to know.

'Beauty is truth, truth beauty,'—that is all
  Ye know on earth, and all ye need to know.

The problem for a reader is to decide who is speaking in the last lines. John Barnard identifies five different interpretations made possible by the different versions of the last two lines: (1) "both lines are spoken by the urn, and addressed to man"; (2) "the lines are spoken by the poet to the urn"; (3) "the lines are spoken by the poet to the figures on the urn"; (4) " 'Beauty is truth, truth beauty' is spoken by the urn, and the remainder is the poet speaking to his readers"; (5) "the motto, as in [the] preceding reading, is spoken by the urn, but the poet then addresses the urn, not mankind" (Keats 1977, 652).

Before interpreting a work of literature, a reader should have before him (at least according to most theories of criticism) a single version of the work in question, preferably a version as reliable as possible. ("Reliable" here means a version that available evidence suggests is as close as possible to the version the artisan, if present, would authorize.) In accidental displacement, one discovers this reliable text by a process of *restoration*, by removing ingredients apparently dropped into the broth by hands other than the chef's. In simple multiplication, one discovers the reliable text by a process of *selection*, a sort of literary game show in which the question to be answered is "Will the real 'Ode on a Grecian Urn' please stand up?"

Complex Multiplication

Perhaps the most difficult case of all is complex multiplication. Here the function that is first multiplied is that of the artisan. As a result of there being multiple artisans, there are also multiple artifacts. Then, as a result of the multiple artifacts, there is usually a displacement in order to resolve the multiple artifacts into a single artifact.

Again the Presocratics provide a good example, but there are also a number of more modern examples, the most striking of which is Ferdinand de Saussure's *Course in General Linguistics*. Saussure gave three courses in general linguistics at the University of Geneva during the years 1906 to 1911. He did not himself publish the content of those lectures, nor apparently was he at the time of his death in 1913 in the process of preparing a manuscript containing the material covered in the lectures. Yet his students considered the content of those lectures fruitful and important; so important, in fact, that certain of his students undertook to prepare the lectures for publication. Unfortunately, Saussure had "destroyed the rough drafts of the outlines used for his lectures" (Bally and Sechehaye 1966, xvii), and only older outlines, which bore little resemblance to students' notes, were found. So the editors were obliged to use as their primary sources the notes of students rather than those of Saussure himself. Certain approaches were considered and rejected. (1) Publish everything in its original form? No, this was impossible because "the repetitions—inevitable in free oral presentation—overlappings, and variant formulations would lend a motley appearance to such a publication." (2) Publish the results of only one of the three courses? No, that would "deprive the reader of the rich and varied content of the other two courses."

(3) Publish "certain particularly original passages without change"? No, "we would be distorting the thought of our master if we presented but fragments of a plan whose value stands out only in its totality." The editors' final solution was, they claim, "bolder" and "more rational": "to attempt a reconstruction, a synthesis, by using the third course as a starting point and by using all the other materials at our disposal, including the personal notes of F. de Saussure, as supplementary sources" (xviii–xix).

So the creative history of the *Course* runs something like this: Saussure himself acts as the arché, and his lectures as the archive. The students whose notes were used all function as artisans, and their notebooks as the artifacts. The editors, Bally and Sechehaye, act as secondary artisans. The published *Course* itself is the secondary artifact. Such a creative history, as the editors were aware, leaves the *Course* open to various criticisms. The most important type is the criticism Jonathan Culler offers in his book on Saussure: He argues that, though "in general they did an admirable job," there were three respects in which the editors were unsuccessful, and Culler sets out in his own book to right those wrongs (1977, 6). What happens in Culler's criticism is that he usurps the role of secondary artisan, he becomes in effect a tertiary artisan, and he makes a creative history parallel to the first and using the same arché, archive, artisans, and artifacts, but resulting in another artifact, the tertiary artifact, which corrects, he claims, the shortcomings of the secondary artifact produced by Bally and Sechehaye.

I would be remiss not to offer, for a single work in which several of these forces are active, a consideration slightly more thorough than has been given in the examples above. The "work" I shall consider is actually a two-work corpus, the *Iliad* and the *Odyssey*. While much of the scholarship to which I must necessarily refer is controversial, what is at issue (the nature of authorship and the explanatory power of the model I have proposed) is, I think, independent of the controversy. I do not hope to resolve all critical debate on the authorship of the *Iliad* and the *Odyssey*; only to illustrate in this concluding section one of the central theses of this book: that authorship is not a single function but a group of related functions, and that these functions cannot in the case of every literary work be attributed to a single individual, except in an arbitrary and misleading way.

The paucity of reliable information about Homer from antiquity has meant that the guessing game of identifying the author of the *Iliad* and the *Odyssey*, and of fixing his dates and the dates of the works, long has been played with makeshift boundaries. These boundaries were fuzzy enough in 1897 to allow even speculations as entertaining as these made by Samuel Butler and here summarized by David Grene:

[Butler's book] tries to establish three main points—all of them in the 1890's rejected by the classical scholars. The first is that the *Odyssey* and the *Iliad* were written by one author apiece, and that a different one. The second is that the *Odyssey* was composed about two hundred years after the *Iliad* and about the year 1050 B.C. The third is that the writer was a young Sicilian lady who lived at Trapani and that the entire locale of the poem is drawn from Sicily— for the author knew nowhere else. (1967, vii)

But Milman Parry's work around 1930, gathered in *The Making of Homeric Verse*, showed conclusively that the Homeric poems were composed orally. Although Parry did not himself play the guessing game of identifying the author of the *Iliad* and the *Odyssey*, with this discovery he did rewrite the rules.

Parry's demonstration that the *Iliad* and the *Odyssey* were composed orally meant that the date of the composition of the poems could no longer be taken as necessarily the date the poems were written down. The upshot, of course, was that evidence for the date of composition could no longer be taken as evidence for the date of writing, and this rendered meaningless not only the "standard" attempts to infer the dates of author and works, but also anomalous attempts like that of Butler (since they too depended on the orthodox assumption that the date of composition must be the same as the date of writing). Parry divided into two questions what had previously been taken as one: now the question about the date of composition is a question about the *creation* of the poems, while the question of the date of writing is a question about the *preservation* of the poems (Cedric Whitman 1965, 5). This means that one of two common assumptions about authors must be given up, at least in the case of the Homeric poems. Either it is not the case that (1) authorship entails, among other things, composing a work and preserving it (writing it, typing it, etc.), or it is not the case that (2) authorship of a given work must always be restricted to a single individual or to collaborating individuals. I argue that the Homeric poems are evidence that the second assumption must go. There are many unresolved issues concerning the origin of the Homeric poems, but for the purpose of establishing the complexity of their authorship only certain of the less controversial facts and the more important questions will be necessary.

Scholarly consensus places the composition of the Homeric poems in the eighth century B.C. G. S. Kirk groups the evidence for the date of composition into these classes:

I. Datable phenomena within the poems themselves
    (i) archaeological criteria
    (ii) language and style

II. Datable external effects of the poems
  (i) datable quotations from and literary references to Homer
  (ii) epic scenes on vases
  (iii) the foundation of fresh heroic cults, possibly as a result of the spread of the Homeric poems
III. The evidence of chronologists in antiquity
IV. The implications of literature and literary personalities in the seventh century

(1962, 282–87)

The different classes, according to Kirk, provide evidence having rather uneven value. Language and style, for instance, are practically no help at all, being unable to suggest a range any narrower than 1000 to 650 B.C. Likewise, datable quotations are no help, as they help to date only heroic poetry in general, not Homeric poetry specifically. The evidence of chronologists in antiquity is more useful; Herodotus puts Hesiod and Homer four hundred years and no more before his time, which would place Homer soon after 850. But by far the most valuable evidence is provided by Arctinus of Miletus, whose *Aithiopis* takes up where the *Iliad* left off. Since Arctinus was born around 744 and his floruit was before 700, Kirk infers that the "monumental composition" of at least the *Iliad* must have been not later than the late eighth century, and could have been earlier. Kirk concludes: "Thus provisionally and with due caution I accept the 8th century, as many others have, as the probable date of composition of the *Iliad*—and probably too, close to its end, of the *Odyssey*" (287).

The date of writing apparently is significantly different from the date of composition. There are two issues here: (1) when it became possible to write down the Homeric poems (when the Greek alphabet originated), and (2) when the first "official" written version appears to have been made. Rhys Carpenter argued in his groundbreaking 1933 article "The Antiquity of the Greek Alphabet" that the Greek alphabet must have been adapted from the Phoenician alphabet around the year 700 B.C. Carpenter's estimate has since been slightly revised by L. H. Jeffery in her definitive book *The Local Scripts of Archaic Greece*. Jeffery concludes that "on the present evidence we might infer that the date of birth [of the Greek alphabet] was somewhere about the middle of the eighth century" (1961, 21). It is important to ask also how quickly the alphabet spread, and when it began to be used for literary purposes. Carpenter offers a schedule for the spread of the alphabet that spans approximately a hundred years before writing became "generally diffused throughout the Aegean and the Greek colonies" (1933, 29). According to Carpenter, "the first recorded effort at longer composition [is] the laws of Zaleukos for Lokri in Southern Italy" in 663 B.C., and it was probably not until at least the following generation that writing began to be used for literary purposes. His speculation that writing was not used for literary purposes until a later period is called into question by the Ischia cup, a Geometric cup found in a cremation tomb in 1954, which D. L. Page says can be dated to the late eighth century and which bears an inscription mentioning the cup of Nestor celebrated in the epic tradition (1956, 95–97). There is no reason to think that the reference to Nestor's cup implies that any portion at all of the poems in the epic tradition were written down by the time of this inscription, but the inscription does indicate the possibility of a transition stage between "dedicatory inscriptions on vases" and "writing used for literary purposes." Still, even if one follows Jeffery in placing the introduction of the alphabet at around 750, and even if one allows for a prodigiously quick transition to the use of writing for sustained literary efforts like the Homeric poems, there is no possibility of the date of composition and the date of writing being coincident.

Tradition tells us that in Athens in the sixth century B.C. Pisistratus exerted some type of influence on the Homeric poems: He put them together or perhaps edited them, and he had them performed by rhapsodes at the Panathenaea. Carpenter claims that the evidence about the origin of the alphabet supports this tradition. Others, though, doubt the tradition's veracity. J. A. Davison argues, against D. L. Page's claim in *The Homeric Odyssey*, that "we ... know that our manuscripts presuppose a standard Athenian text made in the sixth century B.C.," but that "when we enquire into the foundations of this claim, the whole edifice dissolves before our eyes" (1955, 3). Davison argues for at least these two claims: (1) the "standard" text that is the grandfather of our texts of the *Iliad* and the *Odyssey* originated in the second century B.C., probably under the influence of Aristarchus; and (2) the text recited at the Panathenaea was not of Athenian origin, but was imported from Ionia. Davison makes an important distinction between the history and the "proto-history" of our manuscripts of the Homeric corpus. The history proper of our manuscripts begins with the earliest papyrus texts in the third century B.C. The "proto-history" is what we can infer from the extant manuscripts and from "the quotations of 'Homer' in the works of fourth century and earlier authors" (4).

Others, notably G. S. Kirk in *The Songs of Homer*, place more stock in the Pisistratean recension than does Davison, but it is not necessary for our purposes to settle the issue. What is important here is: (1) All parties (tradition, Davison, and Kirk) agree that there was some sort of stabilization of the text into a written version in mid-sixth-century Athens, and (2) Davison's argument that the "Atticized" text that after 150 B.C. was the standard was written in the twenty-four-letter Ionic alphabet, which did not become the standard Athenian alphabet until 403/402, does seem to make it unlikely that "a text written in the full 'Ionic' alphabet could itself be the direct result of the activities of a sixth-century Athenian editor" (5), and to imply that significant forces acted on the text between its "proto-history" and its "history."

There have been attempts to reunite the writer with the composer, based on theories of how the poems were transferred from the spoken to the written word. Maurice Bowra suggests in his *Heroic Poetry* that Homer was an oral poet who learned to write, and thus was able to write down his own composition. In "Homer's Originality: Oral Dictated Texts," Albert Lord denies that there can be any such thing as the kind of "transitional text" for which Bowra argues, that is, one composed orally and then written down by a single individual; Lord argues instead, based on his observations of Yugoslav oral poetry, that the *Iliad* and the *Odyssey* are "oral dictated texts," that is, the illiterate composer dictated the poems to a literate scribe. Kirk points out, though, in "Homer and Modern Oral Poetry: Some Confusions" that all the theories that place the composition and the writing of the *Iliad* and the *Odyssey* in a time of transition from oral to written technique in literature are based on assumptions about "the length and complexity of the Homeric poems, and not on assumptions about Homer's date and that of the introduction of alphabetic writing." To translate this into the terminology introduced above, the arguments for concurrent composition and writing are based on commitments to certain creative modes. Bowra seems to be willing to commit himself at all costs to the real creative mode, uniting the functions of arché and artisan into a single individual, and Lord seems committed to a form of the transcendental mode, in which the function of the arché (oral composition) is not possible for the artisan, but in which the preservation (writing) of the orally composed material is not possible without the artisan.

The available information about the composition of the Homeric poems suggests the following conclusion. If by "Homer" we mean to designate the author of the *Iliad* and the *Odyssey*, we are designating not a blind Greek bard or even a person at all, but a whole nexus of people and forces. The ore and the arché are "ordinary" in the case of the Homeric poems; they do not directly contribute to distinguishing this case from a case that fits the standard model given at the beginning of the chapter. These functions are probably best spoken of as being fulfilled in the case of the ore by the Greek language, Mediterranean geography, and so on, and by the Muses in the case of the arché. But at the archive the case of the *Iliad* and the *Odyssey* stops being "usual." For the function of the archive is fulfilled by the oral traditions that produced the stories of Troy and of Odysseus's wanderings, as well as the formulae used by the bards as their tools to express those stories. Though the stories of Troy and Odysseus have proved useful in a wealth of later literature, the oral formulae had no function in written literature and rapidly disappeared under the influence of writing; in fact, they were so eclipsed by "written ways" of expression that their pervasiveness escaped readers and scholars for centuries. The long process in which the techniques of oral composition were handed down from bard to bard for generations, and in which the poems took shape, is also unusual. The process has two notable features: (1) the multiplication of bards, since the process did not occur in a single chain of bards, one bard at a time; and (2) the displacement involved in what was apparently a process of several centuries. If there was within this process a "monumental composition" (as Kirk suggests there was), it adds another step in the middle of the process for the monumental composer and his artifact. If Kirk is right and there was a monumental composition, it would have to come in the middle of the process of handing down the tradition, since it makes use of a tradition already very rich in history, and since Kirk himself points out that the poems would have had to survive about six generations from the time of monumental composition to the time of writing (1979, 332). Then comes Pisistratus (or whoever is responsible for the sixth-century Athenian stabilization of the text), the artisan responsible for the first "official" version, with another step for the work of Aristarchus (or whoever was responsible for the second-century "official" version). Then the distribution of written versions. And finally, the modern complexities, such as the multiplication of editions and translations.

I have not done justice to the complexity of the authorship of the Homeric poems, but even this cursory glance is enough to show at least two things I have been seeking to establish about authorship. First, it shows that the creative histories of works are various enough that it would be a mistake to try to typify the creative act or to speak of its essence without first coming to terms with the several forces at work within it. And second, it shows that the activities that come under the umbrella of "authorship," even as the term is normally used, need not always be performed (and in fact are not always performed) in the case of a given work by a single individual or even by individuals in willful collaboration.

THREE

The Created Author

Somebody else has arrived. Somebody else is writing.
—Mark Strand

The question of the author's influence on the interpretation of a literary work has been thought of in the past primarily as the question of the relationship between the creative author (or, by synecdoche, the artisan) and the text. The assumption was that the text is a signifier whose proper signified is the meaning intended by the creative author. On that assumption, appropriate problems to be solved by criticism were: What are the techniques by which an author makes known her intention in the work? What sources of information (historical context, author's biography, etc.) are available to aid the reader in ascertaining the author's intention? How can a reader be sure he has ascertained the correct (i.e., authorially ordained) meaning? That "natural" assumption, though, has in this century been questioned with increasing energy, and in fact (at least in the theory of academic critics, if not in popular practice) widely rejected.

The New Critics were among the first to examine seriously the privileging of the creative author's intention. They changed the question from "Given a diversity of possible meanings for a text, *how does* one choose the author's intended meaning?" to "Given a diversity of possible meanings for a text, *why should* one choose the author's intended meaning?" This change involved a corresponding shift from the pursuit of the *correct* interpretation to pursuit of the *best* interpretation. The

New Critics showed that discovering the author's intended meaning for a text is not as simple a task nor one as easily justified as choosing an artisan's intended artifact in a case of simple multiplication. One might offer many reasons to explain the increased difficulty. For example, given the description of the creative author in the previous section, it is apparent that the term "author's intention" is ambiguous. Does it mean the artisan's intention? the archive? the arché's intention? With the advantage of the more precise terminology, one might formulate the New Critical objection as follows: "By the claim that the author's interpretation of a work is not always the best interpretation we mean that the artisan's understanding of the artifact does not always correspond more closely to the archive than that of a reader, who has just as good an opportunity to perceive the archive in the artifact as does the author."

But neither the history of the criticism of the "natural" assumption nor a detailed examination of the New Critical position is in order here. What is most important for the purposes of this section is to note the gravitation toward the claim that "meaning," rather than being born of the artisan's unmediated will and only discovered by the reader through the aid of the text, is a child born of the intercourse between reader and artifact. The artifact is the artisan's child, but that does not make its *meaning* his child as well. The artisan's *descendants*, not his *sons*, will number as the dust of the earth and the stars of the heavens.

In the chapter on the implied author, I will examine two previous studies, one by Wayne C. Booth and another by Jenefer M. Robinson, in order to show how, despite their inadequacies, these studies lead up to an important principle, namely, that just as an artisan creates as many characters as he needs for his purposes (telling a story, proving an assertion, etc.), so a reader, in her interaction with an artifact, creates as many characters as are necessary for her purposes (understanding the text, accounting for what she believes about its history, producing a coherent interpretation, etc.). In the chapter on the created author, I will identify the three most important characters produced by the interaction of artifact and reader; and, through examples, I will study them and their relationships during the act of interpretation.

CHAPTER 7

The Implied Author

Wayne Booth is generally credited with introducing the "implied author" into the menagerie of critical critters, and the implied author has so flourished in its captivity that it has proven to be not merely useful but even important to recent criticism. Booth introduces the implied author in a chapter of *The Rhetoric of Fiction* devoted to debunking what he claims is "the predominant demand [in fiction] in this century," the demand "for some sort of objectivity" (1961, 67). Booth identifies as underlying the term objectivity "at least three separate qualities: neutrality, impartiality, and *impassibilité*" (67). The implied author first appears in the discussion of objectivity as neutrality, and is an integral part of Booth's argument that "no author can ever attain to this kind of objectivity" (68). Booth isolates first the "passion for neutrality" modeled on science and recommended by Flaubert. Quoting Flaubert, Booth says subscribers to this view hold that the author of a fictional work should model his attitude on that of the scientist, "treating the human soul with the impartiality which physical scientists show in studying matter." But, argues Booth, even if this view of science were correct, it still would not provide a good analogue for art, since "we all know by now that a careful reading of any statement in defense of the artist's neutrality will reveal commitment; there is always some deeper value in relation to which neutrality is taken to be good" (68).

Fortunately, however, one need not "dismiss talk about the author's neutrality simply because of this elementary and understandable confusion between neutrality toward *some* values and neutrality toward *all*" (69). The author need not become a "man in general," forgetting his "individual being" and "peculiar circumstances."[1] The author's individuality, Booth claims, is important:

> As he writes, he creates not simply an ideal, impersonal "man in general" but an implied version of "himself" that is different from the implied authors we meet in other men's works. . . . It is clear that the picture the reader gets of this presence is one of the author's most important effects. However impersonal he may try to be, his reader will inevitably construct a picture of the [implied author] who writes in this manner—and of course that [implied author] will never be neutral toward all values. Our reactions to his various commitments, secret or overt, will help to determine our response to the work. (70–71)

Booth makes two other important observations about the implied author (or as Booth, following Kathleen Tillotson, also calls him, the author's "second self"). The first is that for every real author there are various implied authors, "for regardless of how sincere an author may try to be, his different works will imply different versions, different ideal combinations of norms" (71). The implied author varies according to the needs of a particular work, Booth says, in just the same way that "one's personal letters imply different versions of oneself, depending on the differing relationships with each correspondent and the purpose of each letter" (71). The second important observation is that there is an implied author in all fiction, though the implied author may be more noticeable in works where "the second self is given an overt, speaking role in the story" (71, 73).

But Booth's formulation of the concept of the implied author, important though it has been, is not without problems. The most significant of these problems is that Booth typically speaks as though the implied author were willfully created by the real author. A more accurate description of what is actually the case would be to say that the *artifact* is created by Booth's "real author," but that the *implied author* is created not by the real author but by the reader in his interaction with the artifact, so that "inferred author" would be a more accurate name. The "real author" is indirectly responsible for the implied author, by virtue of his having made the artifact in just the way he did, and thereby limiting the possibilities open to the reader; but the fact that different readers produce widely varying impressions of the implied author is evidence enough (given that the real author's action is a constant, which does not vary from reader to reader) that the immediate responsibility for creating the implied author is in the hands of the reader who is interpreting the text.

The real author, to put the situation in another way, may be a necessary cause, but it is the reader's relationship to the text that is the efficient cause. The real author delimits certain possibilities, but if she selects among them in a way that could be spoken of as efficient causation, it is only when she is herself a reader of her own text; she can directly create an implied author only in her role as reader, not in her role as creative author of the artifact. William Blake, for instance, when he wrote "The Marriage of Heaven and Hell," delineated certain possibilities concerning the implied author. The implied author of that work must be acquainted with the Christian religion, and so could not be a Buddhist monk from Tibet in the second century B.C. But there are other conflicting possibilities. The implied author might be someone who believes that he dined with the prophets Isaiah and Ezekiel, or he might be someone who only imagined this without believing it; to make sense of the work, the reader has to decide which of the two it is, and Blake the creative author cannot participate in the decision. Blake himself perhaps *wanted* the reader to choose one or the other, and no doubt chose one in his capacity as reader of his own work; but he did not determine (and could not have determined) in his role as creative author what personality the reader would infer as the "implied author" of the text.

Booth himself, although he cannot do so openly while remaining consistent with his other claims, does implicitly acknowledge the weight of the reader's responsibility in creating the implied author. He claims that, though the fashionable terms for the norms sought in a work may change and though the fashionable terms become misleading if they "come to seem like the purposes for which the works exist," still the reader's search for the norms in a work, whether they are called the "theme," the "meaning," or whatever, expresses an unchanging need:

> Though the old-style effort to find the theme or moral has been generally repudiated, the new-style search for the "meaning" which the work "communicates" or "symbolizes" can yield the same kinds of misreading. It is true that both types of search, however clumsily pursued, express a basic need: the reader's need to know where, in the world of values, he stands—that is, to know where the author *wants* him to stand. But most works worth reading have so many possible "themes," so many possible mythological or metaphorical or symbolic analogues, that to find any one of them, and to announce it as what the work is *for*, is to do at best a very small part of the critical

150

task. Our sense of the implied author includes not only
the extractable meanings but also the moral and emotional
content of each bit of action and suffering of all the
characters. It includes, in short, the intuitive apprehension
of a completed artistic whole; the chief value to which
this implied author is committed, regardless of what party
his creator belongs to in real life, is that which is
expressed by the total form. (73–74)

The implicit acknowledgment, claimed for Booth at the beginning of this paragraph, of the weight of the reader's responsibility in creating the implied author shows itself in several ways
in this passage. There are, Booth says, many possible "themes"
in a work, and part of the reader's task is to *find* one of them.
What is apparently important to Booth is not the real author's
sense of the implied author, but *"our* sense" of the implied
author. And our sense of the implied author is arrived at by
"the intuitive apprehension of a completed artistic whole"; it
is, apparently, the reader's "assembly" of the work through
reading, rather than the real author's "assembly" of it, that
produces the implied author who counts. It is *"this* implied
author," that is, the one created by the reader's intuitive apprehension of the work, that on Booth's account ought to be our
concern, even in preference to the creative author's values "in
real life."

Soon a further problem appears. Booth acknowledges, as
shown above, that there may be various implied authors present
in the works of a single writer. But it is now clear that there is
not only more than one implied author, but more than one *kind*
of implied author, or at least two poles within the conception of
the "implied author"; and Booth does not distinguish between
them, but instead uses the term "implied author" to refer equiv-
ocally to both. In the passage just quoted, Booth speaks of

the implied author as a given reader's "reconstruction" of the source of a work on the basis of the reader's conception of the norms and values embodied in that one work, that single "completed artistic whole." But in the passage (71) where he argues that a single real author will produce works that result in various implied versions of himself, the example of personal letters suggests that two kinds of implied author are being discussed. The first kind, the kind to which Booth gives priority, is what one might call the "singular" implied author. The reader infers this implied author on the basis of a single letter, so that from a letter to a former mistress and an application letter for a job, both written by the same person, one would infer different implied authors. But over against the "singular" implied author is set what one might call the "synoptic" implied author. This implied author is the one a reader infers from a collection of letters.

Booth uses the inclusive sense of his term "implied author" at (for example) pages 75–76. There he agrees with Flaubert that Shakespeare "does not barge clumsily into his works," but disagrees that "we do not know what Shakespeare loved or hated." He says that Flaubert is right on his second point

if he means only that we cannot easily tell from the plays whether the man Shakespeare preferred blondes to brunettes or whether he disliked bastards, Jews, or Moors. But the statement is most definitely mistaken if it means that the implied author of Shakespeare's plays is neutral toward all values. We do know what this Shakespeare loved and hated; it is hard to see how he could have written his plays at all if he had refused to take a strong line on at least one or two of the seven deadly sins. . . . The implied Shakespeare is thoroughly engaged with life, and he does not conceal his judgment on the selfish, the foolish, and the cruel.

True enough, one might say. But what about the implied author of *King Lear*? It seems fair to say that he has a tragic view of life. And the implied author of *A Midsummer Night's Dream*? His view of life is clearly *not* tragic. That much Booth accounts for with his statement on page 71 about "various versions." But the implied Shakespeare of *all* the plays (the one referred to on p. 76) who is "thoroughly engaged with life," and so on, seems to be implied in a different way from the way in which the implied author of *Hamlet* is implied.

Once the two poles of "singular" and "synoptic" implied authorship are brought out, a series of questions present themselves, centered on the question of what constitutes a "completed artistic whole."[2] Should a reader interpreting *Hamlet* concern herself only with the implied author of that play, or should she also (or exclusively?) concern herself with the implied author of all the plays? Why should one speak, as Booth does, of the implied author of Shakespeare's *plays*? What about the sonnets? How do they change our conception of the implied Shakespeare? Is John Berryman's "Dream Song #14" a completed artistic whole? Is 77 *Dream Songs*? Or is only the larger *The Dream Songs* a completed artistic whole? This kind of question necessitates the "mechanisms" I will articulate in the following chapter.

First, it will be useful to consider an application of the notion of the implied author to a specific problem. Booth says, "Three other terms are sometimes used to name the core of norms and choices which I am calling the implied author" (74). The first such term he lists is "style," which Booth says is only one aspect of implied authorship. Jenefer M. Robinson attends to this aspect in her essay "Style and Personality in the Literary

Work." The received view of style carries "such strong overtones of the merely verbal . . . [that it] excludes our sense of the
author's skill in his choice of character and episode and scene
and idea" (Booth 1961, 74). In Robinson's words, "The ordinary
conception of style is that it consists of nothing but a set of
verbal elements such as a certain kind of vocabulary, imagery,
sentence structure and so on" (Robinson 1985, 227). But Robinson attempts to show that style is instead a way of doing
things like "describing characters, commenting on the action
and manipulating the plot," which way of doing things constitutes an expression of the implied author's personality; and as
a corollary, that the verbal features of a work ordinarily thought
of as the whole of style are not in and of themselves stylistic
elements, but are so only insofar as they contribute to the
expression of the implied author's personality.

I argue against Robinson that her essay depends for its success
on a certain conception of authorship, and that this conception
is wrong on at least two counts. First, Robinson's essay, like
The Rhetoric of Fiction, conflates the singular implied author
and the synoptic implied author. And second, by equivocating
on the phrase "is an expression of," her essay blurs the distinction between the creative author and the created author.

Robinson begins by addressing our concept of style "in ordinary contexts." She says that one's style of dressing, working,
speaking, and so on, is "the mode or manner or way" in which
one dresses, works, speaks, and that this style of dressing, working, speaking, "is typically an *expression* of (some features of)
[one's] personality, character, mind or sensibility" (228–29).
She specifies her meaning in this way: "In saying that a person's
way of doing things is an *expression* of that person's traits of
mind, character or personality, I am saying (1) that the person's
way of doing things exhibits or manifests these traits, and (2)
that it is these traits which cause the person to do things in the

154

way they do [*sic*]" (229). As an example, Robinson says that a blush at a party, if it is an expression of the partygoer's timid character, (1) exhibits or manifests his timidity, and (2) is caused by his timidity.

Robinson summarizes her position on expression in this passage, which is a cornerstone of her essay:

> In general, if a person's actions are an expression of her personality, then those actions have the character that they have—compassionate, timid, courageous or whatever—in virtue of the fact that they are caused by the corresponding trait of mind or character in that person, compassion, timidity or courage. In expression, as the word itself suggests, an "inner" state is expressed or forced out into "outer" behavior. An "inner" quality of mind, character or personality causes the "outer" behavior to be the way it is, and also leaves its "trace" upon that behavior. (229)

The operative phrase in the passage is "if a person's actions are an expression of her personality," for one might just as easily assume (as, for example, an existentialist would) that character is not an inner "state," ontologically prior to one's actions, that in its self-expression determines the course or defines the nature of one's actions, but is instead determined by those actions.[3] On this view, one would say not that Bill blushes at parties because he is timid, but that he is timid because (presumably among other things) he blushes at parties. To plead his case, Robinson's opponent might point to a disanalogy with theology. What is at issue here is, after all, similar in form to Socrates' question to Euthyphro, "Is what is pious pious because the gods approve it, or do they approve it because it is pious?" (10a). Robinson says a timid action, if it is an expression of the agent's personality, is timid because the person who does it is timid; her existentialist opponent says a timid person is timid because he does timid actions. The disanalogy with theology is this: While we might (or might not) allow it to be said of a good God that his killing a dozen people for no reason we can understand is good because it was done by God, who is good, we surely would never allow it to be said of an apparently good person that if he suddenly killed a dozen people for no understandable reason his actions were good because they were done by a good person. Instead, we would say that we only thought he was a good person when in fact he was bad, or that he was once a good person but that he is good no longer.

Robinson, then, is excluding from the class of actions that are expressions all acts that are "out of character," a fact that gives her argument the appearance of circularity. Thus, blushing at a party is an expression of the clerk's timidity, but it is not an expression of the big-game hunter's timidity, since he is not timid but courageous. An action is an expression of a trait of an agent's personality if it manifests that trait, and an action manifests a trait of an agent's personality if it is an expression of that trait. Robinson's justification is that "we do not say that a person has a *style* of doing so-and-so unless that person does so-and-so in a relatively consistent fashion" (230). Her example is dress:

> I have a vulgar and flamboyant *style* of dressing only if I consistently dress in a vulgar and flamboyant way. It may be, of course, that my way of dressing differs considerably from one day to the next: yesterday I wore a purple silk pyjama suit, today I am wearing a frilly scarlet mini-dress and tomorrow it will be leather dungarees and a transparent blouse. Despite these differences, however, we still say that I have a consistent way of dressing, because

all my outfits are consistently vulgar and flamboyant. Moreover, my style of dressing is expressive of a particular feature of my personality, namely vulgarity and flamboyance. (230)

One might object, however. What if I wear a tasteful three-piece Bill Blass suit to work one day, faded overalls the next, slacks and a polo sweater the next, and a paisley leisure suit the next? In that case I would be neither consistently vulgar and flamboyant nor consistently conservative. What particular feature of my personality would my style of dressing then express if not my inconsistency? And if I consistently dress in this manner, how can I be said to have the personality trait of inconsistency? Does our courageous big-game hunter's blushing at parties not express any trait of his personality? Would the vulgar and flamboyant person not be expressing a feature of her personality if she wore a tasteful pastel-blue Gloria Vanderbilt dress with a modest string of pearls? The account of style on which Robinson's theory of literary style depends does not answer these questions.

  The problems intensify in Robinson's second section, "The Personality of the Implied Author." After having argued in the first section that literary style is an expression of the writer's personality, she begins the second section with this significant alteration of her thesis: "What is . . . typically expressed by the style of a work is not the personality of the actual author, but of what, following Wayne Booth, we might call the 'implied author,' that is, the author as she seems to be from the evidence of the work" (234). So that, for example, "however querulous and intolerant the actual Tolstoy may have been in real life, the implied author of *Anna Karenin* is full of compassionate understanding." This sudden complication alters her comparison with the ordinary conception of style, for it makes the consideration of acts performed by an author in the composition of a literary work different from the consideration of most other kinds of acts. Typically, "we are justified in making inferences from the way in which people perform actions to the presence in them of certain [corresponding] character or personality traits"; but in the case of literary composition, "although it may sometimes be legitimate to infer from the way these acts are performed to personality traits in the actual author, it is normally the case that the personality expressed by the style of a literary work is not that of the actual author but that of the implied author" (234). Thus, "the personality which leaves its 'trace' on the way [artistic acts in a work] are performed is a personality created and adopted by the author and which may be different from that of the author herself" (235). Robinson claims that her thesis can accommodate the text's being an expression of the actual author's personality *or* the implied author's personality.

How can Robinson claim that it makes no difference to her thesis whether the text expresses the personality of the real or the implied author, that of the querulous and intolerant author of *Anna Karenin* or the compassionate author? Such indifference results, I believe, from failure to distinguish the nature and responsibilities of the creative author from those of the created author. This failure is manifested in Robinson's equivocation on the word "expression." In her first definition, literary style is constituted by the *writer's* way of doing things (like "describing characters, commenting on the action and manipulating the plot"). In this case, when Robinson says that "an author's way of doing these things is an expression of her personality," one could substitute "an author's way of doing these things expresses her personality" or "an author's way of doing these things is a way of expressing her personality." However, Robinson later says, "My thesis has been that the defining feature of a literary work which has an individual style is that the work is an expression of the personality of the implied author, and that what links the diverse verbal elements of style together into a coherent whole is that they all contribute to the expression of this particular personality" (237). Once again, one might substitute the word "expresses" for "is an expression of," to get this formulation of the thesis: "The defining feature of a literary work which has an individual style is that the work expresses the personality of the implied author."

Notice, though, the important difference between the two formulations of the "same" thesis. In the first, it is the author who is doing the expressing, and the text is an expression only in the sense that it is the result of an expressing on the part of the author. It is not that the text expresses the author's personality, but that the author expresses his personality and the text results. But in the second formulation it is the text that does the expressing, and it is the (implied) author that is expressed. Robinson apparently believes that these formulations are equivalent, but I claim that they are not. The writer may express his personality by writing the text, but the text can express only the implied author's personality, not the "real" author's personality. When we speak of a person "expressing himself" or expressing his personality, we mean it in a sense in which he can express only himself. We do not say that "he is expressing her." It is in this way in which, on Robinson's first formulation, the real author expresses himself. But if we are to use the term consistently, we can then say of a text only that it expresses itself, not that it expresses its writer; it expresses its own personality, not that of its writer. The implied author may be a result of the text's expressing itself, in the same way that the text is a result of the writer's expressing himself; but in any case it surely cannot be that the writer is a result of the text's expressing itself.

Consider Robinson's own example. We may say of *Anna*

Karenin that it is an expression of (the real) Tolstoy's querulousness and intolerance if he wrote it because he felt that all previous European novels were pitiful and idiotic scribblings by pitiful and idiotic men, and that he alone was capable of producing a masterpiece that would never be surpassed. In that case *Anna Karenin* would be an expression of Tolstoy's querulousness and intolerance in the sense that Tolstoy vented his querulousness and intolerance by producing the book. But in the second sense of "expression," *Anna Karenin* would *not* be an expression of (the real) Tolstoy's querulousness and intolerance, for the book itself does not express querulousness and intolerance, but "compassionate understanding." The only author implied by the book is a compassionate, understanding one.

As a result of this equivocation, Robinson, like Booth, experiences difficulty with the singular implied author/synoptic implied author distinction. She claims that "the style of an oeuvre, just like the style of an individual work, is an expression of the personality of the implied author of that oeuvre" (236). But in the same paragraph, attempting to account for variety of style within an oeuvre, she says:

> Just as we sometimes find a variety of styles in a single work (like *Ulysses*), so it is possible to find in a single oeuvre a variety of styles corresponding to radically different implied authors. But in the normal case the implied author of different works is recognizably the "same person." *Of course no two works do or even can express exactly the same personality,* but there will normally be striking similarities. (236–37; my emphasis)

So Robinson has claimed (1) that "a literary work which has an individual style is . . . an expression of the personality of the implied author," (2) that "an oeuvre . . . is an expression of the personality of the implied author of that oeuvre," and (3) that "no two works do or even can express exactly the same personality." From these premises, the conclusion must follow that the personality of the implied author of an oeuvre cannot be exactly the same as that of the implied author of any work within that oeuvre, much less all the implied authors within the oeuvre. Robinson is able to account for variations in style within a work by distinguishing the narrator from the implied author, and allowing the narrator's style to be different from the implied author's; but she offers no similar distinction to account for the variations in style she acknowledges as necessarily present in an oeuvre.

So it is that the personality expressed in the Cyclops scene in *Ulysses* is on Robinson's account that of the narrator (since it is different from the work as a whole), and the personality expressed in the whole work is that of the implied Joyce. But the style of the implied author of *A Portrait of the Artist as a Young Man*, the style of the implied author of *Ulysses*, and the style of the implied author of the oeuvre of which those two works are parts, though they are by her own admission different, in Robinson's essay are all three "Joyce's style."

The concept of the implied author is an important step in the direction of an account of the created author. But I have tried by an examination of Booth's and Robinson's work to show that the concept of the implied author as it has so far been presented is inadequate. In neither of the two works is a satisfactory procedure given for distinguishing between the implied author of a work and the implied author of the oeuvre of which the work is a part, nor is there an explanation given of the relationship between the two. Further, Booth and Robinson both shuttle in their discussions between attributing creative and created functions to the implied author (for example, speak-

ing at times as if the implied author were responsible for creating the work), and fail on that account to maintain consistently
the distinction between the creative author and the created
author. What is needed is an account of the created author that
provides for such important distinctions as the implied author
of a work as distinguished from the implied author of an oeuvre,
and that provides a way of maintaining more consistently the
distinction between the roles of the creative author and the
created author. In the following chapter I will attempt to provide such an account.

CHAPTER 8

The Created Author

I argued in the previous chapter that more than one kind of "implied author" or "author-character" is available to the reader in her attempt to produce a coherent reading, and that the concept of the implied author as it has been formulated by Booth and used by Robinson does not account for all of those "author-characters." In this chapter I will distinguish three such "author-characters" and pursue their ramifications, concluding with an example of their relevance to the interpretation of a philosophical text. I hope in this way to show that the created author, like the creative author, is not a simple, homogeneous entity, but a complex concatenation of forces, and that the activity of this group of forces is central to the interpretation of texts.

The three "author-characters" that result when the reader interprets the artifact are the narrator, singular proxy, and synoptic proxy.[1] The *narrator* is a speaking character within the story (or poem or whatever). There may be any number of narrators in the trivial sense that there may be any number of characters in a story with "speaking parts," or in the more important sense that there are four narrators in *The Sound and the Fury*. The narrator may be closely identified with the "author" of the work, or he may be given an identity of his own, as in, say, one of Browning's dramatic monologues. The *singular proxy* and the *synoptic proxy* correspond very roughly to what in my criticism of Booth and Robinson I called the singular implied author and synoptic implied author, though I will try in this chapter to show some important respects in which they differ.

One of the most important respects in which the created author as I am trying to portray it in this chapter is different from the implied author Booth describes is that Booth takes the implied author to be primarily the responsibility of what he calls the "real author," but I contend that the created author is more directly attributable to the reader and artifact. Booth says that as the real author writes, "*he creates* . . . an implied version of 'himself' " and that "the picture the reader *gets* of this presence is one of *the [real] author's* most important *effects*" (1961, 70; my emphasis). The implication is that the real author is in active control of the picture of the implied author that the reader passively receives. The real author puts the implied author into the text as he writes, and the implied author then reveals himself to the reader unchanged.

The implied author thought of in this way is put into the text in much the same way that the real author might add another word that would then appear unchanged to the reader. It may be true, if one grants the assumptions of a monistic view in which the creative author's intention is the sole determinant of the uniquely correct meaning of a text, that the implied author a reader *ought* to see in the text is put into the text in this way; but I have argued against those assumptions in my criticism of essays by Nehamas in an earlier chapter. I suggest that, suspending the question of what created author the reader *ought* to see (or whether there *is* a single created author the reader ought to see), the created author the reader actually *does* see is put into the text not in the way a word is added but in a manner similar to the way a meaning is added. The real (creative) author has a certain amount and a certain type of control over meaning and over the created author, but he is not sovereign. The reader is essentially a passive receptor as regards the creative author's words,[2] but she is a participant (with power that rivals or perhaps even exceeds that of the creative author) in the creation of meaning and of the created author.

In order to fill out the makeshift definitions given for the meanings of the new terms (narrator, singular proxy, synoptic proxy) introduced above, I will consider examples in which they are clearly distinct from one another. The ways in which the terms separate themselves will fall into patterns, two of which I shall call "schizoscription" and "proxy privilege."

Schizoscription

In schizoscription the narrator is set against one or both of the proxies (in some cases the proxies will be clearly distinct, in others not); at least two separate voices, in other words, are active in the text. The reader attributes one meaning, usually "the literal meaning," to the narrator, and another, "deeper" meaning to the proxy. There are two important kinds of schizoscription, satirical and allegorical.

Satirical Schizoscription
In satirical schizoscription the proxy opposes the narrator. The narrator says one thing, but the reader takes the proxy to mean another.[3] A perfect example of this kind of schizoscription is a satire like Swift's *A Modest Proposal*. Various attempts have been made to explain the way in which satire functions. Northrop Frye calls satire "militant irony," that is, irony with clear moral norms, and with "standards against which the grotesque and absurd are measured" (1957, 223). He says that irony can consistently maintain "complete realism of content" and "the

suppression of attitude on the part of the author" (224). How-ever, satire "demands at least a token fantasy, a content which the reader recognizes as grotesque, and at least an implicit moral standard." Frye concludes that satire "breaks down when its content is too oppressively real to permit the maintaining of the fantastic or hypothetical tone. Hence satire is irony which is structurally close to the comic: the comic struggle of two societies, one normal and the other absurd, is reflected in its double focus of morality and fantasy" (224).

This "struggle of two societies" could also be thought of as a struggle of two levels of awareness, a struggle that has been described in two different ways. The first way is to refer to irony as "the narrowness of the character's vision as revealed by the more inclusive vision shared by author and reader" (Zimmerman 1983, 68).[4] The second way is to accord the user of ironical language "an awareness of irony that is not necessarily less complex than our own." Here "irony is a simultaneous aware-ness of contrarieties by a single consciousness." The first, ac-cording to Everett Zimmerman, is a characteristic way of ex-plaining irony in narrative, and makes the narrator "a character in a tale that defines him"; the second is a characteristic way of explaining irony in polemic, and makes the narrator "an authorial figure who defines the tale" (69).

Both of these ways of describing the struggle between two levels of awareness, though, can be captured in the notion of satirical schizoscription, which asserts that satire and irony work on a disparity between the level of awareness of the narra-tor and that of the proxy, whose level of awareness is equivalent to that of the reader. Zimmerman's first explanation amounts to an emphasis on the narrator's narrowness of vision, and a fairly close identification with the proxy on the part of the reader. The reader, in other words, identifies himself with the "higher" vision of the proxy, and is able on that account to take a condescending position regarding the narrator's vision. Zimmerman's second explanation is, given the notion of satirical schizoscription, only a shift of emphasis to the synoptic proxy. On this explanation, as Gardner Stout puts it, we get "an image of Swift, sitting with his fellow wits in an Augustan drawing room . . . and personating [a Wotton, a Bentley, etc.], while simultaneously carrying on an ironic . . . running commentary on their absurdities" (Zimmerman 1983, 69). The synoptic proxy is the single consciousness in which the contrarieties of the singular proxy (the commenting Swift) and the narrator (the "personating" Swift) are simultaneously present.

Satirical schizoscription works out in *A Modest Proposal* something like this. The narrator is the "I" who offers the proposal that the children of the poor Irish families "be offered in sale to the persons of quality and fortune through the kingdom" to be served as culinary delicacies, and the effect of the work depends on his being naïve enough to be sincere. As Frye puts it, "one is almost led to feel that the narrator is not only reasonable but even humane; yet the 'almost' can never drop out of any sane man's reaction, and as long as it remains there the modest proposal will be both fantastic and immoral" (1957, 224). It is the "almost" that creates the proxy, for though the narrator must be sincere for the piece to work, no sane person would believe the "author" to be sincere. And the "author" who is neither naïve nor without ironic intent is the proxy.

Notice, though, that the narrator and the proxy are not given as individuals prior to the reading of the work; instead, they emerge as individuals in the course of the work. In *A Modest Proposal*, the individuation takes place quickly. The first two paragraphs lay out the problem at hand, a problem both narrator and proxy are concerned with. But in the last sentence of the second paragraph (in which it is suggested that whoever could find a way to make the children of poor people an asset to the commonwealth should "have his statue set up for a preserver of the nation"), the process of differentiation has begun by this identification with the great ironist Socrates; and by the time the heart of the proposal is reached, the narrator and the proxy are completely separate. The narrator relates his discovery that a young, healthy child at a year old is "a most delicious, nourishing, and wholesome food," while the proxy by his very silence lends to this discovery its heavy satire.

Notice, also, that the reader does not take the narrator by himself to say one thing and mean another. Just as Don Quixote must be taken as sincere in his madness in order for Cervantes to be able to satirize romances, so the narrator of *A Modest Proposal* must be taken as sincere in his own kind of madness in order for Swift's satire to work. It is not the narrator, but "Swift himself," that is, the proxy, who is taken to mean something other than what is said. This helps to explain why New Criticism seldom engaged works like Swift's: Without the realization that "Swift himself" is a figure created by the reader and not the historical writer of the text, and with a strict admonition to exclude the intention of the historical writer from determining the meaning of the text, there is no satisfactory way to explain the manner in which satire functions.

I have spoken so far of the function of satirical schizoscription as primarily an opposition between narrator and proxy. This is its defining feature, and is sufficient to explain the functioning of a work like *A Modest Proposal* without making the further distinction between the two types of proxy. That is not to say, though, that there is no distinction to be made between the singular proxy of *A Modest Proposal* and the synoptic proxy of Swift's corpus. (Indeed, as I have mentioned above, one of Zimmerman's ways of explaining the functioning of satire is "covered" by using this distinction.) It does, however, point to an important fact about the three "author-characters," namely, that the terms "narrator," "singular proxy," and "synoptic proxy" designate not fixed classes whose members are defined by a set of common characteristics and whose borders are rigidly fixed, but instead describe a set of basic tensions, shades of gray. The two poles are that of a fictional character entirely within a work, and the actual creative author responsible for the work (and in that sense completely outside it). Between the two poles, the synoptic proxy is closest to the real creative author, the narrator is closest to a fictional character, and the singular proxy is in the middle.[5]

The narrator occupies the part of the spectrum between the character pole and the singular proxy; this is the space of tension between the involvement of a character and the detachment of a singular proxy. For instance, the speakers in Ring Lardner's "Haircut" and J. D. Salinger's *The Catcher in the Rye* are near the character pole. Their vision is closely tied to their place within the story; they are not able to "rise above" the story or to step outside of it for a broader perspective. At the other extreme would be the narrator in a philosophical treatise, like the "I" of Kant's *Critique of Pure Reason*, whom the reader takes to be as detached as possible ("objectivity" being one of the goals) and hardly distinguishable from the singular proxy. Suspended in between would be someone like Marlow in *Heart of Darkness*. He is clearly given as a character, since his story is quoted at length by another "I," with even some commentary by the "I." Yet there is not much evidence to distinguish his vision from that of the proxy. So, one might say that "Haircut" tries to merge the narrator with the character pole, that the *Critique of Pure Reason* tries to eliminate the character pole altogether and merge instead the narrator and singular proxy, and that *Heart of Darkness* tries to blur the distinction between the character pole, narrator, and singular proxy.

The singular proxy occupies the part of the spectrum between the narrator and the synoptic proxy; this is the space of tension between being inside and outside the work. In a case like Kant's *Critique*, where the narrator and the singular proxy are practically indistinguishable, the proxy operates by involvement. All that is relevant about the proxy is explicit within the work. But in a case like *A Modest Proposal* or Browning's "Johannes Agricola in Meditation," where the narrator and the singular proxy are not only distinguishable but at odds with each other, the proxy operates by his absence. Nothing about the proxy is explicit within the work; he is inferred by the reader from what the narrator says (combined of course with the reader's own knowledge of the world, understanding of language, etc.).

And last, the synoptic proxy occupies the part of the spectrum between the singular proxy and the pole of the real creative author; this is the space of tension between the fictional and the real. One might also think of this as the tension between what is inferred from within the artifact and what is inferred from outside the artifact. There are two basic ways in which the synoptic author separates himself from the singular author. The first has been noted above, in the discussion of *The Rhetoric of Fiction*, as the difference between the "singular implied author" and the "synoptic implied author," where the information from outside the artifact comes from within an oeuvre. Thus, a reader might infer a "Shakespeare" (a singular proxy) on the basis of her reading of *A Midsummer Night's Dream* that would not be the same as the "Shakespeare" (synoptic proxy) she infers after reading several other comedies plus the major tragedies. The other primary way in which the synoptic author separates himself from the singular author is on the basis of outside information, such as historical or biographical information, which colors the way the reader interprets. An example of this has been the reaction to Hemingway's work in the wake of his suicide. The stories and novels value courage and machismo, but Hemingway's suicide has been taken by many as evidence of a lack of courage and manliness on his part. Hemingway is thus perceived as not "practicing what he preaches"; his manner of ending his life is thought of as inconsistent with what was taken as the achievement of his work. Thus the factual information about the way Hemingway ended his life has so altered the (synoptic) proxy inferred from outside his works that many readers now view the (singular) proxy inferred from within the works as unbelievable or insincere.

It is important to note that this way of setting up the tensions is potentially misleading in at least one respect: The character pole can be, and frequently is, reached. Narrators are, in cases like *The Catcher in the Rye*, very strictly characters. However, the pole of the real creative author is an ideal but is not attainable, even in the case of living authors. Even a reader who knows a living author personally can hardly be said to have an accurate re-creation of that author at her command in interpretation.

Allegorical Schizoscription

In satirical schizoscription, as shown above, the proxy opposes the narrator. In allegorical schizoscription, however, while it is still the case that the narrator says one thing and the proxy is taken to mean another, the proxy's meaning is taken not as opposing but as supplementing or deepening the narrator's words. The reader, that is, attributes a more or less literal meaning to the words and connects that meaning to the narrator; she also attributes a deeper, typically figurative, meaning to the words and connects that meaning to the proxy. This form of schizoscription is important because it has been a pervasive influence on the reading habits and critical theories of our culture. The assumption that what an author *says* (what the narrator literally means) and what he *means* (what the proxy figuratively means) are typically different, or that a text has a surface meaning and a deeper meaning, is so common that it often goes unnoticed and unexamined.

One of the best examples is found in St. Augustine's principles of scriptural interpretation in *On Christian Doctrine*. There Augustine sets out the basic distinction between literal and figurative meaning as a logical outgrowth of his distinction between signs and things. Things (in the strict sense) are what is not being used to signify something else, while signs are things which are being used to signify something else. Augustine presents the literal/figurative distinction as a sort of second-order parallel: The things signified on a literal reading do not themselves further signify, but the things signified on a figurative reading do further signify. Knowing when an expression is literal and when it is figurative is for Augustine an important skill, essential to proper interpretation, and requiring "no little care and industry" to practice. "He who follows the letter takes figurative expressions as though they were literal and does not refer the things signified to anything else." But this is a dangerous mistake because "there is a miserable servitude of the spirit in this habit of taking signs for things, so that one is not able to raise the eye of the mind above things that are corporal and created to drink in eternal light" (1980, III, v, p. 84).

The Jewish people, according to Augustine, were in such servitude, but their servitude "was different from that of the others, since they were subjected to temporal things in such a way that the One God was served in these things." For "although they took signs of spiritual things for the things themselves, not knowing what they referred to, yet they acted as a matter of course that through this servitude they were pleasing the One God of All whom they did not see" (III, vi, p. 84). That is, the Jews acted in such a way that their behavior had one meaning for themselves, based on their own intentions and limited knowledge, and another meaning for God, based on his own intentions for them and his unlimited knowledge. Given that assumption, Scripture (thinking for now of the Old Testament), as a record of the history of the Jewish people and a revelation of God's working through them, will have two levels of meaning: one, the literal, corresponding to the human view; and another, the figurative, corresponding roughly to the divine view.

That the levels of meaning, human and divine, correspond respectively to the literal and the figurative is attested by Augustine's criterion for determining whether a locution is literal or figurative. Generally, Augustine says, the method "consists in this: that whatever appears in the divine Word that does not literally pertain to virtuous behavior or to the truth of faith you must take to be figurative. Virtuous behavior pertains to the love of God and of one's neighbor; the truth of faith pertains to a knowledge of God and one's neighbor" (III, x, pp. 87–88). There are two possibilities: Either the human and the divine levels of meaning may coincide, or they may differ. In the first case, the locution in question is to be taken literally. In the second case, since the divine purpose is to be preferred, the locution must be taken in such a way that it harmonizes with the divine; and since it does not do so literally, it must be read figuratively.[6] There are then two intentions at work. One of them, however, is in control of the other, so that even when the human intention produces a meaning that is not literally that of the divine intention, the divine intention is able to use the human intention as a figure for the divine meaning. The divine meaning deepens, revises, or supplements the human meaning.

The result of all this is not as complicated as it may sound.

Since the Jews seldom were aware of the divine meaning of their actions (laboring as they were in servitude of spirit), Augustine advocates an allegorical or "apostolic" method of reading the Old Testament, claiming that "all or almost all of the deeds which are contained in the Old Testament are to be taken figuratively as well as literally" (III, xxii, p. 98). If we are to understand the divine meaning of the Scripture, if in other words we are to understand the Scripture as revelation and not merely as history, we must on Augustine's view learn to discover the proxy's view behind the narrator's words. An example of this principle put into practice is found at II, vi. There, as part of his answer to the question of the value of similitude in Scripture, Augustine reads Song of Solomon 4:2 as a passage praising the Church metaphorically as if it were a beautiful woman:

> "Thy teeth are as flocks of sheep, that are shorn, which come up from the washing, all with twins, and there is none barren among them"[.] Does anyone learn anything else besides that which he learns when he hears *the same thought* expressed in plain words without this similitude? Nevertheless, in a strange way, I contemplate the saints more pleasantly when I envisage them as the teeth of the Church cutting off men from their errors and transferring them to her body after their hardness has been softened as if by being bitten and chewed. I recognize them most pleasantly as shorn sheep having put aside the burdens of the world like so much fleece, and as ascending from the washing, which is baptism, all to create twins, which are the precepts of love, and I see no one of them sterile of this holy fruit. (37–38; my emphasis)

Augustine claims that, although the divine meaning would be the same even had it not been presented through figuration, still "no one doubts that things are perceived more readily through similitudes and that what is sought with difficulty is discovered with more pleasure" (II, vi, p. 38). The Scriptures were written as they were (with the divine meaning typically given figuratively) in order to "deceive those who read casually" and to "conquer pride by work and to combat disdain in our minds" (II, vi, p. 37).

The Augustinian method of interpretation allows for a given passage to have more than one meaning, and for a given passage to have a meaning other than that intended by the person who wrote it. The operative principle is that God is the author of all of the passages in the Bible, and that he is perfectly capable of producing a meaning (such as the prefiguration in the Old Testament of what was to come in the New) without depending on the human writers of Scripture to share his intention. I contend that this method of interpreting Scripture is analogous to the way in which any reader interprets a work that she takes to have a "deeper" or "symbolic" meaning behind the literal, surface meaning. She discerns in the text two intentions at work, privileges one of them as the dominant one, and attributes the dominant intention to the proxy and the other intention to the narrator.

In Augustine's interpretation of Scripture, it happens that (1) the important tension is between the synoptic proxy and the narrator, rather than the singular proxy and the narrator,[7] and (2) the two intentions are attributed to two clearly distinct individuals, one of whom (God) has a claim to dominance on the grounds of his divinity. But neither of the two need be the case. In Yeats's "The Wild Swans at Coole," for instance, the tension is between the singular proxy and the narrator, and the two individuals are not as obviously distinct (since neither is named, and certainly neither is a divinity). But it is not for those reasons any less the case that two intentions are at work in the poem, as even a textbook New Critical interpretation shows. Brooks, Purser, and Warren talk of the poem as an "apparently objective and simple bit of description" and also of "the implied contrast [of the poet] with the swans," by which contrast Yeats, they say, suggests "*symbolically*, an existence outside time, unlike that of man, who is trapped in time, and in memory" (1975, 359). So there is on their view one explicit descriptive intention and one implicit symbolic intention; and although Brooks, Purser, and Warren want to identify both intentions with the historical Yeats himself, even their reading depends on the distinction between what I have called the narrator and the proxy.

Schizoscription, then, is one of the ways in which the important differences between the three "author-characters" make themselves felt. Schizoscription is typically a function of the difference between the narrator and the (undifferentiated) proxy; although, as has been shown above, it may at times be a difference between the narrator and either the singular proxy or the synoptic proxy specifically, or it may even be a difference between the two proxies. At any rate, it is a functional difference between two of the author-characters. In satirical schizoscription, the two are at cross-purposes, and in allegorical schizoscription the two work together, with one deepening or supplementing the other.

Proxy Privilege

There is another way, in addition to schizoscription, in which the important differences between author-characters make themselves felt. This second way is typically a function of the difference between the singular proxy and the synoptic proxy, and I refer to it as "proxy privilege." There are, as one might expect, two kinds, depending on which proxy is privileged.

Synoptic Proxy Privilege

This is the standard case in respect of an oeuvre. In synoptic proxy privilege, the synoptic proxy is of the two proxies the dominant one in the interpretation of a work within the oeuvre. The synoptic proxy is likely to dominate whenever the oeuvre is seen as reasonably consistent. Already a good example, Shakespeare, has been encountered above in the discussion of *The Rhetoric of Fiction*.

Booth argues that Flaubert was wrong in his claim that "we do not know what Shakespeare loved or hated." Booth says that, at least for the implied author of Shakespeare's plays, we do know a great deal about what he loved and hated. "The implied Shakespeare is thoroughly engaged with life, and he does not conceal his judgment on the selfish, the foolish, and the cruel" (1961, 76). But, as I argued above, the implied author (singular proxy) of *King Lear* does not seem to be the same as the implied author (singular proxy) of *A Midsummer Night's Dream*, nor does he seem to be the same as the implied author (synoptic proxy) of the plays collectively. But if there is a difference among these proxies, then it is legitimate to ask whether a reader of *Lear* should concern herself only with the singular proxy of that play, whether she should concern herself only with the synoptic proxy of the oeuvre, or whether there is some intermediate position that is best.

In an instance of synoptic proxy privilege, like Booth's comments on the implied Shakespeare, the answer (whether given after conscious consideration or not) to the question of which proxy should dominate in interpretation is, as the name synoptic proxy privilege indicates, the synoptic proxy. When reading *Lear*, one does not speak of it as a testament to Shakespeare's tragic view of life, for one assumes that the purpose of this play must be compatible with the purpose of *A Midsummer Night's Dream* (i.e., capable of being thought of as having proceeded coherently from the same pen), and the latter play clearly could not be a testament to a tragic view of life. Since synoptic proxy privilege is the standard assumption, one need not read far to find other examples. The first sentence of David Bevington's introduction to *King Lear* in his edition of the plays says, "In *King Lear*, Shakespeare pushes to its limit the *hypothesis* of a malign or at least indifferent universe in which man's life is meaningless and brutal" (Shakespeare 1980, 1168; my emphasis). Shakespeare, according to Bevington, does not "demonstrate his belief that the universe is malign or indifferent," nor does he "paint a vivid picture of a malign or at least indifferent universe," either of which might be said of the singular proxy. Instead, he pushes a *hypothesis* to its limits; and the reason it can only be a hypothesis is that Bevington considers the most important author-character of *King Lear* to be the one who also wrote *The Merry Wives of Windsor* and *The Tempest*, namely, the synoptic proxy.

But although synoptic proxy privilege is common, and is generally taken, without argument, as obviously applicable, there are also frequent instances in which the synoptic proxy is not, and apparently should not be, dominant. These I call, of course, instances of singular proxy privilege.

Singular Proxy Privilege
Regarding the question of whether she should concern herself strictly with the singular proxy of the work in question, or strictly with the synoptic proxy of the oeuvre, or whether there is some intermediate position that is best, in a case of singular proxy privilege the reader answers by giving priority to the singular proxy. This will normally occur when works within an oeuvre are seen as irreconcilable, as for instance when an author disavows an early work. In a case of singular proxy privilege, any attempt to bring the interpretation under the

influence of the synoptic proxy is secondary; that is, it is posterior to, and has no determining influence on, the interpretation.

Consider Nietzsche's early book *The Birth of Tragedy*. In it he
argues vehemently that the Apollinian/Dionysian opposition,
"by a metaphysical miracle of the Hellenistic 'will,' " ultimately generates "an equally Dionysian and Apollinian form
of art—Attic tragedy" (1968, 33). And he argues that what he
calls "aesthetic Socratism," which is embodied in the works of
Euripides and which follows the principle "To be beautiful
everything must be intelligible" (83–84), is responsible for the
destruction of the tragedy born by the Apollinian/Dionysian
struggle. What is of particular interest here, though, is not *The
Birth of Tragedy* alone, but *The Birth of Tragedy* considered
together with Nietzsche's own later comments on it.

The Birth of Tragedy itself first appeared in 1872, followed
by a second edition "with very slight textual changes [which]
was printed in 1874 and appeared in 1878." By 1886, though,
Nietzsche's views having changed significantly, "the remaining
copies of *both* editions were reissued," but now prefaced by
an "Attempt at a Self-Criticism."[8] The "Attempt at a Self-
Criticism" amounts to an explicit disavowal of certain ideas
(or ways of formulating ideas) in *The Birth of Tragedy* and a
reinterpretation of others. Here are a few excerpts from his self-
criticism:

> Whatever may be at the bottom of this questionable book,
> it must have been an exceptionally significant and
> fascinating question, and deeply personal at that. (17)

> What I then got hold of, something frightful and
> dangerous, a problem with horns but not necessarily a
> bull, in any case a new problem—today I should say that it

was the problem of science itself, science considered for the first time as problematic, as questionable. (18)

I do not want to suppress entirely how disagreeable it now seems to me, how strange it appears now, after sixteen years—before a much older, a hundred times more demanding, but by no means colder eye which has not become a stranger to the task this audacious book dared to tackle for the first time: *to look at science in the perspective of the artist, but at art in that of life.* (19)

What found expression here was anyway . . . a *strange* voice, the disciple of a still "unknown God," one who concealed himself for the time being under the scholar's hood, under the gravity and dialectical ill humor of the German, even under the bad manners of the Wagnerian. (19–20)

Such statements are problematic for the following reason. Synoptic proxy privilege is a way of describing an assumption readers typically make about the manner in which the interpretation of one work within an oeuvre is influenced by the other works in the same oeuvre. But Nietzsche's "Attempt at a Self-Criticism," itself a work within the same oeuvre as *The Birth of Tragedy*, influences the interpretation of *The Birth of Tragedy* precisely by excommunicating it, by saying that it is not to influence or be influenced by the rest of the oeuvre. In the case of Shakespeare, one assumes that all the plays Shakespeare wrote are harmonious at least in the sense that, just as they were produced by a single hand, so they produce a single (synoptic) proxy. It is this assumption that charges the Shakespearean synoptic proxy with his power as a force in interpretation, for it rules out any interpretation of a single work that is inconsistent with the synoptic proxy. But Nietzsche's "Self-Criticism" forces a different assumption about *The Birth of Tragedy*, since it is an explicit statement that the works are not harmonious, that they were in a very important sense not produced by the same hand (note that Nietzsche refers to "the muser and riddle-friend who was to be the father of [*The Birth of Tragedy*]" almost exclusively in the third person), and that therefore they should not yield a single synoptic proxy.

One way to think of the change from the more typical synoptic proxy privilege to singular proxy privilege is as a shift in the burden of proof. Normally, given two competing interpretations, the one that is more closely compatible with the other works of an author will be preferable unless a compelling reason can be given for choosing the other. The burden of proof, in other words, is on the interpretation that is apparently less compatible with the rest of the canon. But Nietzsche's "Attempt at a Self-Criticism" shifts the burden of proof as regards competing interpretations of *The Birth of Tragedy* from the apparently incompatible interpretation to the apparently compatible one. It would be possible to assert that *The Birth of Tragedy* is one with the later works in a more direct sense than as a "foreshadowing" or "prefigurement" of certain dominant concerns, but to do so would require a defense against the words of the "Self-Criticism."

To say that *The Birth of Tragedy* is "excommunicated" is clearly an oversimplified account of its relationship to the rest of the Nietzschean canon, and perhaps raises more questions than it answers. For instance, the "Self-Criticism" does not establish clearly whether *The Birth of Tragedy* is to be entirely isolated, or whether it is to be grouped with other early works, like "Philosophy During the Tragic Age of the Greeks," into a sort of early sub-oeuvre separate from the later works.[9] And I have not dealt with such important questions as whether and how a relationship of foreshadowing and prefiguration is different from the "typical" relationship of works in an oeuvre. However, I hope that the distinction between synoptic proxy privilege and singular proxy privilege, if it is not in itself capable of offering neat solutions to problems like that surrounding *The Birth of Tragedy*, will at least draw attention to the important and frequently unexamined question of how and to what extent works within an oeuvre should influence one another's interpretation.

One way in which an author can enforce singular proxy privilege without disavowing a work, and without the works in an oeuvre necessarily being seen as irreconcilable by the reader, is through the use of pseudonyms. Louis Mackey says as much in his discussion of Kierkegaard's use of pseudonyms:

> The distinction between pseudonymous and direct writings establishes the independence of the poetic production [the pseudonymous writings]. Because they can be opposed to the known intent of Kierkegaard, the works of the pseudonymous *personae* are protected against biographical and psychological snoopery. Neither symptoms nor simulacra of any living person, they stand by themselves and take their autonomous literary effect. (1971, 249).

Mackey's argument is that by themselves only the direct writings need correspond to "the known intent of Kierkegaard" (i.e., the intent of the synoptic proxy). Kierkegaard is "a kind of poet" partly because the pseudonyms dictate that the pseudonymous works be read as one would read a soliloquy in a play rather than as one would read a critical essay: We demand of essays that they "express their author's views" (i.e., that the singular proxy be identifiable with the synoptic proxy), but we do not expect this of soliloquies (we do not demand that Hamlet always say what Shakespeare himself believes). So one result of Kierkegaard's use of pseudonyms is that they enforce singular proxy privilege. The pseudonymous works, like Hamlet's soliloquies, may be part of an overall plan associated with the synoptic proxy (as Mackey claims), but they cannot be read as direct expressions in themselves of the synoptic proxy.

One sphere in which proxy privilege is especially important is textual criticism. It appears there in two main ways, which might be called "earlier privilege" and "later privilege." In earlier privilege, the assumption is that, all other conditions being the same, the older a manuscript is, the more preference it is to be given in assembling or reconstructing the text; the earlier the proxy, in other words, the more "authentic" he is assumed to be. An example of earlier privilege is biblical manuscripts. Because of the manner in which they were copied and distributed, one assumes that, all other things being equal, the older the manuscript is, the more accurately its proxy approximates the actual creative author. In later privilege, on the other hand, the assumption is that, all other conditions being the same, the later the manuscript, the more it is to be preferred in interpretation. An example of this is Walt Whitman's *Leaves of Grass*, which between 1855 and 1892 went through nine editions with significant revisions. Here the assumption is that the latest version, which represents the actual creative author's wishes at the time of his death, is the most authentic. It has been argued often that earlier versions are better for one reason or another; but any such argument amounts to saying that this earlier version is the one the author *should have* preferred, and no such argument can remove itself from the shadow of Whitman's words, "In the long run the world will do as it pleases with the book. I am determined to have the world know what I was pleased to do" (1975, 21).[10]

The interesting question raised by the distinction between singular proxy privilege and synoptic proxy privilege is not whether there are instances where the singular proxy should have more weight in interpretation than the synoptic proxy; indeed, there are enough cases like the *Tractatus* and *Philosophical Investigations*, where it is difficult to imagine what a synoptic proxy might look like, to answer that question before it is asked. The interesting question is to what extent the synoptic proxy is a projection from the reader of the same desire for static personal identity in others that causes disappointment at the sight of old girlfriends at high school class reunions: "She's just not the same girl I remembered." It is a natural enough tendency. Emerson says in a famous passage from "Self-Reliance" that to be great we must fight against demanding such strict consistency of ourselves or allowing others to demand it of us:

> A foolish consistency is the hobgoblin of little minds, adored by little statesmen and philosophers and divines. With consistency a great soul has simply nothing to do. He may as well concern himself with his shadow on the wall. Speak what you think now in hard words and tomorrow speak what tomorrow thinks in hard words again, though it contradict everything you said today.— 'Ah, so you shall be sure to be misunderstood.'—Is it so bad then to be misunderstood? Pythagoras was misunderstood, and Socrates, and Jesus, and Luther, and Copernicus, and Galileo, and Newton, and every pure and wise spirit that ever took flesh. To be great is to be misunderstood. (1968, 95)

Michel Foucault asks that his readers not demand it of him: "I am no doubt not the only one who writes in order to have no face. Do not ask who I am and do not ask me to remain the same: leave it to our bureaucrats and our police to see that our papers are in order. At least spare us their morality when we write" (1982, 17). And the distinction between synoptic proxy privilege and singular proxy privilege advises the reader of a given work to consider whether and to what extent the demand for a synoptic proxy may in that case be the hobgoblin of little readers, an expression of the "bureaucratic morality," causing the pure and wise work to be misunderstood.

Proxy Revision

Proxy revision occurs when a proxy is able to influence the shape of the artifact (by which I mean not only the artifact *qua* artifact but also the meaning attributed to it) in such a way that she strengthens her own claim to authority (against the claims of other possible proxies). Since this is most apparent in cases where the authenticity of at least part of a text is in question, the fragments of Heraclitus, the status of many of which (as direct quotation, testimony, forgery, etc.) is unclear, will provide a vivid example of proxy revision.

As mentioned earlier, the Presocratic philosophers are all notoriously sticky cases of authorship because they are instances of complex multiplication (the fragments having been transmitted to us within the works of multiple artisans), and at least some of the fragments are also apparently victims of systematic displacement. In the case of Heraclitus, more than twenty-five different artisans have preserved one or more of the fragments now considered authentic. And there are other problematic facts about the authorship of Heraclitus's fragments. For instance, one of the fragments says, "It is wise, listening not to me but to the [*logos*], to agree that all things are one."[11] Our sources of the extant fragments attribute them to Heraclitus (putting him in the role of arché for the fragments as we have them), but here at least it appears that Heraclitus attributes the important content not to himself but to the *logos*, effecting a displacement of sorts so that the *logos* becomes the authority behind the authority of Heraclitus, the arché behind the Heraclitus who is arché for the existing fragments.

But the most interesting aspect of the authorship of the fragments of Heraclitus, and the aspect that is of primary interest here, is the relationship of the proxy to the fragments. I have shown above that the proxy is always created by the reader's interaction with the text, but in the case of Heraclitus the proxy himself helps to create the very text by which he is created, by being one of the standards against which dubious fragments are tested for authenticity, or against which different versions of a fragment are tested in order to select a single authentic version. The fragments of Heraclitus are, in other words, an example of proxy revision, as the following comparison of three important scholarly editions of the fragments will show.

Consider, for example, the fragment numbered 51 by Diels and Kranz. Kahn translates it: "They do not comprehend how a thing agrees at variance with itself; it is an attunement turning back on itself, like that of the bow and the lyre." Kirk, following Zeller, emended homologeein to sympheretai. Zeller had argued "that the ms. reading homologeein is a mistake caused by the occurrence of this verb twice in the preceding two sentences, and that an original sympheretai (or xympheretai) should be restored from two Platonic passages, one of which certainly and the other probably refers to this fragment."[12] But Kirk says that "quite apart from Plato, homologei does not seem suitable" (1954, 205). He argues that, although homologei in fragment 50 ("Listening not to me but to the Logos it is wise to agree that all things are one" [Kirk's translation]) "has a special meaning which is partly dependent on the hidden word-play between

-logein and logos: the sense is 'it is wise to listen to the Logos and to say-the-same-as-the-Logos, that all things are one,' " there is no such motive in fragment 51. "On the contrary, Heraclitus was by no means averse from using cognate forms with opposed prefixes to express strictly opposed ideas, and [therefore] sympheretai *is what we should expect* after diapheromenon, as in fr. 10" (my emphasis). Kirk also emends palintropos in favor of palintonos, largely (though not exclusively) because "palintonos is a Homeric word, like many in Heraclitus's vocabulary" (213). The item of interest here is the extent to which in deciding what Heraclitus *has said* Kirk depends on a prior notion of what Heraclitus *should say*, given Kirk's understanding of Heraclitus (i.e., his Heraclitean proxy).

Marcovich follows Kirk in both emendations, though not for the same reasons. For the first, he says only that "I think homologei . . . is due to some Stoic version of the fragment" (1967, 124). "Sympheretai is the preferable reading, because Plato . . . uses this word although homologei would better suit his purpose" (125). For the second, Marcovich offers six different reasons, the first two (and the weightiest) of which are similar in their dependence on a prior proxy to Kirk's reasons for the same change. First, Marcovich, quoting Verdenius, says that "palintonos is a current epithet of the bow," which is almost exactly the same as Kirk's claim that palintonos is a Homeric word and there are many such Homeric words in Heraclitus's vocabulary. The difference is an understood premise. Marcovich's claim could be expanded to something like this: Palintonos is a Homeric epithet of the bow, Homeric epithets were current in the vocabulary of Heraclitus's time, Heraclitus's vocabulary was the vocabulary of his time, and so on. Second, Marcovich points to the implication of tension in -tonos, claiming that this better accords with the diapheromenon and sympheretai in this fragment and also with fragment 80.[13] So

Marcovich, like Kirk, depends for his editorial decisions at least in part on a proxy formed prior to those decisions, enabling that proxy to establish more firmly his claim to be "the real Heraclitus."

As an editor and a commentator, Charles Kahn is the most self-conscious, and consequently the most interesting, of the three. He cannot escape proxy revision, but in a chapter called "On Reading Heraclitus" he makes explicit many of his assumptions about Heraclitus and the most important of his principles of interpretation, and he also demonstrates his awareness that "in principle the effort to recover the authentic Heraclitus, that is, to attain a uniquely correct interpretation, is an enterprise that can never succeed" (1979, 87). He says that "every age and philosophical perspective, from Cratylus to the Neoplatonists and the fathers of the Church, projected its own meaning and its own preoccupations onto the text of Heraclitus." And even though there is no "timeless vantage point from which a uniquely true picture of Heraclitus might be obtained," we are, he claims, at least responsible to choose an interpretive framework deliberately, so that we do not "become unconscious and hence uncritical prisoners of whatever hermeneutical assumptions happen to be 'in the air' " (88).

Kahn says that his aim is to "emphasize the double significance of Heraclitus' achievement: as a literary artist and as a philosophical thinker of the first rank." His method of achieving that aim will be to focus on the "intimate connection between the linguistic form and the intellectual content of his discourse" (89). I argue that (1) Kahn's statement of his aim is essentially a description of his Heraclitean proxy, (2) that this description does not simply result from a post-editorial interpretation of the fragments, but that the proxy is himself a shaping force in the editorial decisions that shape the fragments, and (3) that the proxy's influence is always a self-confirming one. In other words, I argue that, in spite of its being more self-conscious regarding critical procedure, Kahn's book, like the others, is a clear example of proxy revision.

Kahn adopts as a starting point three assumptions: linguistic density, resonance, and meaningful arrangement. The third assumption is in two parts: "(1) I assume that the original order was a meaningful one, and (2) I assume that the order I have chosen is true to Heraclitus' own meaning." His explanation of what he means by the first two assumptions is worth quoting at length.

> By *linguistic density* I mean the phenomenon by which a multiplicity of ideas are expressed in a single word or phrase. By *resonance* I mean a relationship between fragments by which a single verbal theme or image is echoed from one text to another in such a way that the meaning of each is enriched when they are understood together. These two principles are formally complementary: resonance is one factor making for the density of any particular text; and conversely, it is because of the density of the text that resonance is possible and meaningful. This complementarity can be more precisely expressed in terms of 'sign' and 'signified', if by *sign* we mean the individual occurrence of a word or phrase in a particular text, and by *signified* we mean an idea, image, or verbal theme that may appear in different texts. Then density is a one-many relation between sign and signified; while resonance is a many-one relation between different texts and a single image or theme. (89)

Linguistic density and resonance, according to Kahn, result in "a prose style which fully justifies Heraclitus' reputation as 'the obscure' *(ho skoteinos)*" (95).

Kahn rejects the emendations of Kirk and Marcovich, and his reasons are telling. Of the first emendation, he says that Zeller's original proposal to change from homologeein to sympheretai was a result of his being "insensitive to the imagery and flexibility of Heraclitus' language," and that the emendation's acceptance "by a whole generation of recent editors" is "one of the strangest phenomena in Heraclitean scholarship" (195). As for the second emendation, Kahn says that the choice of *palintonos* is an attempt "to avoid (rather than to resolve)" the riddle of "the enigmatic epithet *palintropos*" (199). But "the solution to this puzzle," Kahn says, "is obvious, *once we grasp the allusive nature of Heraclitus' style and his systematic use of resonance*." (my emphasis). Density helps to determine the choice between variants, because "by Homeric reminiscence, *palintropos* immediately suggests *palintonos*," and "hence the former term is richer, since by association it includes the latter as well." But resonance also helps, because -*tropos* "provides a direct allusion to the 'turnings' or 'reversals' (*tropai*) of fire in [31], and hence to their more familiar parallel, the seasonal turning back of the sun in summer and winter [suggested in 94]."

So the Heraclitean proxies of Kirk and Marcovich, with their Homeric vocabularies and propensity for using cognate forms with opposed prefixes to express strictly opposed ideas, dictate that fragment 51 must be read with sympheretai and palintonos, while Kahn's Heraclitean proxy, with his predilection for resonance and density, dictates that homologeein and palintropos are preferable. But Kahn's proxy is not satisfied with helping to choose between variants in the fragments. He has developed such a reputation for ambiguity and obscurity that he is able to render any unambiguous text not backed by dependable sources doubtful or inauthentic, and he does just that to a doxographical account of the logos in Sextus Empiricus. Kahn says of the

"physical identification of the 'common *logos*' with the circum-
ambient atmosphere or *pneuma*" that it is unsupported by evidence from the fragments and that

> this doctrine is also un-Heraclitean in its unambiguous
> precision: it states a psychophysical theory which happens
> to be false, but which some ancients believed to be true.
> But it preserves no hint of that poetic resonance and
> density that make Heraclitus' own statements . . .
> profoundly meaningful for a modern reader, who can no
> longer take seriously the ancient theory stated in the com-
> mentary. (295)

So Kahn and the fragments have created a proxy who could not
merely have stated with "unambiguous precision" a theory
now known to be false and no longer "profoundly meaningful
for a modern reader," and who is not only shaped by the text
but helps to shape the very text by which he is shaped.

Here one might object that, given the state of the extant
testimony about Heraclitus and his work, there is no way to
avoid such circularity. But that is the point: There *is* no way
around proxy revision. This is not in itself a criticism of Kahn
or any of Heraclitus's other modern commentators; it is only a
step toward showing that proxy revision is not limited to such
obviously troublesome cases of authorship as Heraclitus. The
reason that troublesome ancient texts like the Heraclitean fragments suffer more openly than others is that in such texts the
proxy influences not only the meaning attributed to the text
but also the very text itself, while in a more typical case of
authorship the proxy influences only the meaning. Yet in all
cases of proxy revision the proxy is able to influence some
textual value in such a way that she strengthens her own position as "the right proxy." The difference between the "stan-

dard" case and a case like that of Heraclitus is that the influenced value is different; in the former instance the only value influenced is *meaningfulness* or *significance*, and in the latter instance not only the significance but also the *authenticity* or *canonicity* of a text is influenced.

Proxy revision is an alteration of what Heidegger and his followers have called the "hermeneutic circle."[14] Gadamer describes the hermeneutic circle in this way:

> A person who is trying to understand a text is always performing an act of projecting. He projects before himself a meaning for the text as a whole as soon as some initial meaning emerges in the text. Again, the latter emerges only because he is reading the text with particular expectations in regard to a certain meaning. The working out of this fore-project, which is constantly revised in terms of what emerges as he penetrates into the meaning, is understanding what is there. (1975, 236)

I contend that what is initially projected by the reader, even before "an initial meaning emerges in the text," is a set of limits, a range of possibilities, imposed by the reader's prior conception of the author (i.e., the proxy with which the reader approaches the work), even if this is the first work the reader has seen by the author in question.[15] An initial meaning emerges as the reader enters the text; if this initial meaning is within the limits imposed by the proxy, it strengthens his position, narrowing the range of possibilities; if the initial meaning is outside of the limits imposed by the proxy (if it disappoints the reader's expectations), then the proxy must change to accommodate this meaning. This tug-of-war between proxy and text (whose one rule is that proxy and text must always be compatible) continues until the reader leaves the text. Proxy revision occurs when a meaning "emerges *only* because" of the expectations of the reader, when one possibility (a meaning or a textual variant) is chosen over another because the first possibility is compatible with the proxy as he is, while the second possibility would demand that he change.

FOUR

Post-Mortem

it would be enough for me to know
who is writing this
                    —W. S. Merwin

p.
on
6v.

CHAPTER 9

The Book with
a Shattered Author

W hether one finds Derrida's work appealing or appalling, whether one considers him ingenious, disingenuous, or insidious, at least one aspect of his work is undeniably compelling. He has drawn our attention to a serious problem in the way Western literature and philosophy have taught us to think. That Derrida's solution has proven unpalatable to many does not make the problem go away. The problem is this: Western thought, according to Derrida, relies and is structured in terms of pairs of opposites, "good vs. evil, being vs. nothingness, presence vs. absence, truth vs. error, identity vs. difference, mind vs. matter, man vs. woman, soul vs. body, life vs. death, nature vs. culture, speech vs. writing" (Johnson 1981, viii). These pairs of opposites have at least two characteristics: (1) Neither term in a pair is independent; rather than existing by itself, it "belongs to a systematic chain"; and (2) the pairs are "never the face-to-face of two terms, but a hierarchy and an order of subordination" (Derrida 1972, 329). One term is always the corrupted, lessened, or meretricious version of the other: Error is the corruption of truth, woman is a diminished version of man, culture is a prostitution of nature. Derrida's overriding concern is with two of the pairs of opposites, absence vs. presence and speech vs. writing, and his solution, which he calls deconstruction, has two purposes: (1) to overturn a given pair of opposites, thereby neutralizing the privilege of one term over the other; and (2) to undermine the opposition itself (to "displace the system").

A. R. Luria's *The Man with a Shattered World* draws attention to another pair of opposites Derrida discusses: inside vs. outside.[1] Previous views of the author have always been grounded in this pair of opposites, but Luria's book calls those views of the author into question by turning the author/reader/ text relationship "inside out."

Wherever the dichotomy appears, the inside is the privileged member of the pair, the outside its diminished derivative.

- In contexts where the concern is knowledge and understanding, the inside is always the place of acquisition or possession of knowledge and understanding, while the outside is the place of ignorance. We say, for example, "I'd like to get inside his head" or "The thief knew the password, so it must have been an inside job." Our word for transmitting knowledge, to "instruct," comes from the Latin prefix *in-*, meaning "inside," plus the verb *struere*, meaning "to build or pile up," so that the word's original meaning is "to build in."
- In contexts centering on experience, inside connotes possession of experience and outside connotes lack of it. We say "She's really in the know" or "He was really getting into it." Or, conversely, "He won't remember anything; he's really out of it."
- In contexts of power or mastery, the powerful are inside, the weak outside. So someone has "the inside track" or is "in the driver's seat." To intimidate is the same Latin prefix *in-*, combined with *timidus*,

meaning fear, so that to intimidate is to put fear into
someone.

- Our tradition's use of sexuality is connected with the
  inside/outside pair, so that penetration in our culture
  is an act of conquest for the male and acquiescence by
  the female, and for a male to have intercourse with a
  female is to "know" her, with all the inside/outside
  baggage knowledge carries.

- As regards will and purpose, we say that she is "in
  control" or, conversely, that the car went "out of control." Contexts involving reason give us "He's not in
  his right mind" and "He's out of his mind"; wisdom,
  the colloquialism "She's in tune with the situation."

And so on.

This privileging of the inside also dictates where literary
critics have placed the author. Traditional criticism says, pre-
dictably, that the author is inside the text. The author is *inspired*, he *expresses himself in* the text. He turns himself inside
out. He pulls himself out of himself, and puts himself into what
he has produced. The text is the woman who comes from his
own rib, and who is fecund only when he penetrates her. Thus
Shakespeare can write in sonnet 74, "My life hath *in* this line
some interest, / Which for memorial still with thee shall stay,"
and William Gass (who could be more traditional?) can write
an essay called "The Soul *Inside* the Sentence." Contemporary
critics like Barthes, who rebel against the tradition, say just the
opposite: The author is *out*side the text. Both traditional and
recent anti-traditional criticism, though, assume that the inside
is the place of privilege and power. Even when Derrida says
"there is nothing outside the text," he does not mean that the
author is inside the text, only that because he is outside he is
nothing. *The Man with a Shattered World* implicitly undercuts

the assumption that the inside is the place of privilege and power, and shows that authority need not come from the inside.

The Man with a Shattered World is a chronicle of the twenty-five-year doctor/patient relationship between A. R. Luria, an eminent Russian neuropsychologist, and Lyova Zasetsky, once a promising young engineering student in the third year of his studies at a polytechnic institute, who had been shot in the head during World War II, at the battle of Smolensk in 1943. The German bullet lodged in the left posterior parieto-occipital region, resulting in physical symptoms that included destruction of local tissue, atrophy of the medulla, adhesion of the brain to the meninges, damage to the left lateral ventricle, inflammation of the brain, and the formation of scar tissue.

The neuropsychological consequences were tragic. A few examples from his numerous symptoms:

- Zasetsky suffered after his wound from what Luria elsewhere calls "contralateral homonymous hemianopia" (1973, 107–8), a condition in which the right side of his visual field was "an even gray vacuum" (1987, 37). Further, objects in the left half had become fragmented, and "ceased to resemble complete entities."
- His perception of his body was distorted. He would frequently lose awareness of the right side of his body, or misperceive proportions: "Suddenly I'll come to, look to the right of me, and be horrified to discover half of my body is gone," and "Sometimes when I'm sitting down I suddenly feel as though my head is the size of a table . . . while my hands, feet, and torso become very small" (42–43).
- He lost his spatial orientation and sense of direction, so that he could no longer chop wood or use a hammer, and he was unable after his wound to walk

by himself even in his hometown, within blocks of his home, without being lost.

The list of Zasetsky's symptoms is long, but one set of those symptoms in particular fascinates Luria, and proves important to the study of the author. Zasetsky was able to write, and during his association with Luria composed a journal of more than three thousand pages, portions of which are reproduced in the book (in juxtaposition with Luria's writing), yet his wound had left him unable to read what he had written.

Immediately after his wound, he was completely illiterate. The type on the newspaper "seemed familiar" (63), but Zasetsky, although he recognized the photograph of Lenin, did not recognize the letters as Russian characters and could not read them. With the help of a teacher Zasetsky tried to learn to read again, but it took "a few months" (68) just to learn the alphabet, and he "still couldn't identify any of the letters immediately" (68). Even after he had mastered the letters, though, he was unable to acquire any facility at reading. Such a small portion of his visual field was intact that he could take in no more than three letters at a time, and he "[had] to focus a little to the right and above a letter in order to see it" (68). So for the rest of his life he read letter by futile letter, word by futile word.

If I want to understand a word, I have to wait until the meaning comes to me. Only after I read a word and understand it can I go on to the next word, and then the third. By the time I get to the third word I often forget what the first or sometimes even the second word meant. No matter how hard I try, I just can't remember. (69)

In spite of his inability to read, though, Zasetsky could write. He was unable to write deliberately, self-consciously, letter by letter, so that initially both he and Luria thought he had lost all ability to write. At their first meeting, Luria asked Zasetsky to write his own name, but this "led to a desperate struggle. Awkwardly he picked up the pencil (by the wrong end at first), then groped for the paper. But . . . he could not form a single letter" (18). Later, however, it was discovered that he could write automatically, "spontaneously, without thinking" (73). Luria's explanation for Zasetsky's ability to write automatically without being able to write deliberately is straightforward. Writing deliberately, as a child would, relies on visualizing each letter, and reproducing on paper the visual image. But Zasetsky's vision and spatial perception were damaged by his injury. Automatic writing, on the other hand, "is an automatic skill [that adults acquire], a series of built-in movements which I call 'kinetic melodies' " (72); and Zasetsky's "kinetic-motor functions," the ones controlling such "kinetic melodies," remained intact.

Luria's explanation for Zasetsky's ability to write without being able to read what he had written is slightly more complex, but no less important. Luria divides the brain into three basic functional units (1973, 43–101; 1987, 22–35). The first is the unit for regulating cortical tone: It is located at the base of the brain, in the upper parts of the brain stem and the reticular formation, and it determines whether the brain is awake or asleep, and how alert the brain is. The second unit is for obtaining, processing, and storing information: It "includ[es] the visual (occipital), auditory (temporal), and general sensory (parietal) regions" (1973, 67), and is responsible for contact with the outside world. The third unit is for programming, regulating, and verifying mental activity: It is located in the anterior portion of the brain, and "creates *intentions*, forms *plans* and *programmes* of . . . actions, inspects their performance, and *regulates* . . . behaviour so that it conforms to these plans and programmes; finally, [it] *verifies* . . . conscious activity" (1973, 79–80). It was the second unit that was damaged in Zasetsky.

The fact that the second unit was destroyed while the other two remained intact is what for Luria lends to Zasetsky's case its interest and its tragedy. That the portions of the brain that plan and that maintain alertness were left intact meant that Zasetsky was able to work at his writing with extraordinary determination and perseverance. For twenty-five years, his work was unflagging: "I work on this story about my illness from morning until five in the evening while my mother and sisters are out working. . . . Sometimes I'll sit over a page for a week or two. . . . I work at it like someone with an obsession" (81). And the writing, though automatic, was not easy. "Although he learned to write quickly and automatically, this was a far cry from being able to express his ideas in writing. To do so he needed words and these did not come easily: he had to rack his brain in order to put together a sentence that would convey his idea" (76). That the portion of the brain that monitors and verifies mental activity was intact meant that he was painfully aware of his deficiencies. He knew the suffering that it caused his family, and he was able to enumerate and analyze the very failures of language and memory and understanding that he was unable to overcome. That the portion of his brain that operates the memory and regulates contact with the world was irreparably damaged meant that his situation was hopeless. Luria says, "Had he understood his dilemma from the start, life would have been unbearable" (91). Unlike most of the body's cells, nerve cells do not regenerate. The destruction was permanent. Luria describes in this way the paradoxical state that resulted:

A split . . . had formed because some brain functions had remained intact while others had been destroyed completely. Hence, though he was unable to grasp the point of a simple conversation, or of many grammatical constructions, he left us an amazingly precise description of his life. It required superhuman effort for him to write one page of this journal, yet he wrote thousands. Despite his inability to cope with elementary problems, he was able to present a vivid account of his past. Furthermore, he still had a powerful imagination, a marked capacity for fantasy and empathy. (155)

The peculiar symptoms that result from the second unit's being destroyed while the others remain intact are also what makes *The Man with a Shattered World* such an illuminating case of authorship, since it alters the inside/outside relationships. Because he cannot even read what he has written, Zasetsky is an outsider to his own work. Luria tries to use Zasetsky's journal, in relation to which Zasetsky is always an outsider, in order to get inside Zasetsky's mind. Yet, even though in that sense Zasetsky is the paradigmatic outsider to his own writing, in another he is quintessentially inside. He cannot regulate his memory, cannot call up thoughts or words or reminiscences at will, so his memories are in a curious way more nearly present in the journal than in himself, though he no longer has access to them there. He is in his journal rather than in himself. Zasetsky's journal is in Luria's book, published in Luria's name, in Luria's order, and with Luria's interpretations. Luria is an outsider to Zasetsky; Zasetsky is an outsider to his own text, to the story of his own life; only the bullet penetrates, only the damage is inside Żasetsky.

The Man with a Shattered World shatters a myth: the myth that origin in one individual entails perpetual consolidation there. In that sense, it is a concrete illustration of the New Critical view that the writer is not the definitive reader: Zasetsky in fact was not a reader at all. It also illustrates one of Roland Barthes's claims in "The Death of the Author," namely, that writing is the destruction of the point of origin. Zasetsky's writing "completely drained" him (xix), quite literally, for it took his memories out of himself and out of his own reach. Luria says, "Writing was his one link with life, his only hope of not succumbing to illness but recovering at least a part of what had been lost" (xix–xx), but writing was also a loss of his life, a guarantee of losing anything he recovered. Yet, *The Man with a Shattered World* is more than a proof-text for the New Critics and Barthes.

The New Critics hold that the writer is not the definitive reader, or in other words that his intentions do not determine what the text means, but they do believe that his intentions determine at least what the text says. But Zasetsky is not in control of even that. When he wants (intends) to say something, he cannot call up the words with which to say it.

> Some vague, peculiar, incomprehensible thought would flash through my mind all of a sudden. . . . I'd try to say something, but it was beyond me. All my ideas and vocabulary had escaped me completely. . . . Every time I tried to talk or remember anything it was an endless struggle for words. I still can't think of particular words when I want to talk or think something through. (92–93)

Not only the words to express a thought or memory were out of his conscious control, but the thoughts or memories themselves. Not only could he not choose to express an idea the way he wanted to express it, but he could not choose the idea that he wanted to express. "Images of his past emerged clearly and in great detail, which is why he managed to write this journal. But he could not summon them at will. . . . If someone named an object, he could not immediately get an image of it; when he finally managed to, it . . . lacked the intricate associations memories generally have" (97).

Any attempt to impose order on the ideas he wished to communicate resulted in their dissolution. Just as the physical process of handwriting had to be automatic and not deliberate, so the mental process of composition had to be automatic and not deliberate. If he tried to choose the way he wanted to say something, it would disappear: "Fragments of words swarmed through his mind, colliding with and blocking each other, so that in the process of trying to formulate an idea he forgot what he wanted to say" (119). Or again:

> An idea for something occurred to me, an image of what I wanted to say, and I began to try to remember the right words to express this. No sooner had I got two words down when the very idea that had just taken shape in my mind suddenly disappeared. I forgot what I wanted to write. I looked at the two words I'd written but couldn't remember what I intended to say. So my idea was gone—I couldn't remember it, no matter how hard I tried.
> When a good idea came to me I'd no sooner pick up a pencil than it would be gone. (121)

If Zasetsky illustrates Barthes's claim that writing is the destruction of the point of origin, he also provides a counterexample to the view Barthes uses that claim to support, namely, that language overpowers the author and exiles him from the text but leaves the reader able to penetrate the text. For language overpowers Zasetsky when he reads or listens no less than when he writes. "I only manage to grasp a little of what is said. As soon as I recognize the meaning of a few words, the rest are drowned in the flow of speech I hear" (116). When he read or was read a text in which the narrative flow was interrupted by details and images, he could not "add up [the details and images] to a meaningful context." His comprehension was "restricted to undeciphered images" (118). Just as he could not call up at will the words for a meaning he wished to express, so he could not call up at will the meanings for a word he had encountered.

> Every word I hear seems vaguely familiar. . . . I know a particular word exists, except that it has lost meaning. I don't understand it as I did before I was wounded. This means that if I hear the word "table" I can't figure out what it is right away, what it is related to. I just have a feeling that the word is somewhat familiar, but that's all. (105)

But if Luria was outside Zasetsky's mind, and if Zasetsky was outside his own work; if Zasetsky was, in all our usual ways of thinking of control, not in control of what he wrote; if Zasetsky is so clearly not an author in the usual sense of the word that Luria thinks himself modest to call Zasetsky "the real author" of the book; that does not diminish the book's power. It is a moving book, a book that conveys knowledge, a book with drama, a book that is much richer than this chapter indicates, and whose richness is not due only to Luria. But that very richness enforces the lesson I have tried to articulate: that in literature, criticism, and the practice of reading, we are mistaken to privilege the insider. Zasetsky shows us that the *inside* is not always the place of *insight*. Origin in an individual does not entail consolidation there, and meaning and beauty need not be consolidated at the origin of a text to be present in the text. Meaning and beauty need not have their locus *in* the writer. Purpose, wisdom, understanding, and experience may also be found—and communicated—by the outsider.

CHAPTER 10

"Hiding Pieces of Light They Have Stolen"

If the incidence of plagiarism is not on the rise, irresolution in the face of it is. Not many years ago, Hemingway could have the narrator in "I Guess Everything Reminds You of Something," on discovering his son's first story in "a book of very good short stories by an Irish writer" (1987, 600), render a judgment both immediate and unforgiving: "Now he knew that boy had never been any good" (601). Yet when presented with specific accusations of plagiarism, neither the academy nor the public seems able to render any judgment at all; there is no consensus on what counts as plagiarism or how to tell whether there is really anything wrong in a given case. Blame for the increasing academic and public confusion about and irresolution in the face of plagiarism is often placed on recent trends in literary theory, notably on changing attitudes toward aspects of authorship like creativity. One way, then, of assessing the practical consequences of my attempt to deny the "assumption of homogeneity" and to initiate a change in the way authorship is understood is to ask what view one should hold about plagiarism if my portrayal of the nature of authorship is accurate. Some recent literary critical theories have said of themselves or had it said of them that they would, if correct, entail that plagiarism is acceptable or necessary; but my analysis of the author does not entail that conclusion.

Peter Shaw draws attention to "the literary world's failure to render judgment" in cases of plagiarism by comparing it with "the draconian code imposed by the scientific community" (1982, 325). He cites an example of a scientist who plagiarized sixty words and faked some data in a medical paper and "was asked to leave" his position at Yale when he was caught. Even his superior, who was not himself accused of plagiarizing or faking data, was forced to resign his position (as chair of the department of medicine) at Columbia. Shaw contrasts this to a list of noted literary figures who have been accused of plagiarism, including Norman Mailer, Alex Haley, John Gardner, Ken Follett, and Gail Sheehy, "none of [whom have] suffered from the resultant publicity," not even "those of them who confessed" (325). Plagiarism, on Shaw's view, "has come to be regarded as a relative phenomenon—one to which disgrace no longer attaches" (327).

But as Ari Posner has shown in a recent essay, this tendency to condone plagiarism is not restricted to the literary/academic community. The practice of plagiarism, especially in the form of unacknowledged ghostwriting, is widespread among public figures, especially politicians, and its practice by these public figures has come to be taken for granted:

> From politicians to business leaders, judges to sports figures, our public discourse is carried forward on the backs of a battalion of anonymous scribes. Leaders in nearly every profession depend on helpers to put words in their mouths. Even journalists are getting into the act and hiring assistants to write their columns. If college or high school students relied on ghosts the way most public figures do, they'd be expelled on charges of plagiarism. The

fact that they bought the words rather than stole them would not be considered a defense. (1988, 1-I)

But Shaw and Posner do not agree only about the alleged fact of increasing condonation of plagiarism; they agree also on the consequences of that fact. Both assert that condoning plagiarism devalues writing. Shaw says:

> Today it is difficult to imagine a plagiaristic act, or indeed any other breach of literary ethics, that would go undefended. It hardly seems an accident that along with this particular devolution, literature, in general, went from a position where it could claim for itself the highest morality to one in which many are claiming that it is no more than a marginal entertainment. (336)

And Posner:

> Misrepresentation is so central to our society—in everything from advertising to politics—that it seems a bit feeble to cavil about phony bylines. Everybody knows that Bill Cosby doesn't really eat Jell-O and Cybill Shepherd hates beef. Why be picky about truth-in-packaging for words? On the other hand, the addiction to ghostwriting symbolizes a broad decline in the value of words and of the thoughts that underlie them. (6-I)

Harold Bloom disagrees. Bloom asserts that plagiarism is not only morally acceptable under certain conditions, but necessary to the creation of literature under any conditions. If Shaw and Posner agree on one fact (that condonation of plagiarism is increasing) and one consequence of that fact (that condonation of plagiarism devalues writing), Bloom argues for a different fact and a different consequence. Bloom's alleged fact is that "good poems, novels and essays are webs of allusion, sometimes consciously and voluntarily so, but perhaps to a greater degree without design. This unknowing allusiveness, carried far enough, can become quotation, and no writer ever can be certain precisely when he is quoting" (1982, 413). The consequence Bloom derives from this given is that, since plagiarism is a necessary element of creativity, "the literary question in regard to supposed plagiarism therefore should always be: What is the quality of the stolen material?" Far from devaluing literature as a whole, plagiarism, if done properly (i.e., if one plagiarizes from good sources), increases the quality of the individual work in which it is used.

In order to arbitrate between these views, it will be necessary first to ask what plagiarism is. Producing a good definition is no easy task. Lord Goodman calls it "a deliberate use of a piece of someone else's intellectual property," which in a legal sense "can only mean something that breaches copyright," and in a moral sense "means something that makes use of somebody else's efforts and exertions." Ian McEwan says it is "to claim as uniquely yours what is uniquely someone else's and is a tacit admission that your own imagination is defective, insufficient to sustain its own peculiar hold on the world" (1982, 413). Shaw defines plagiarism as "the wrongful taking of and representing as one's own the ideas, words, or inventions of another" (327). But none of these definitions by itself is complete. Documented quotation in research is "a deliberate use of a piece of someone else's intellectual property" (assuming with Goodman that writings are intellectual property), and "makes use of somebody else's efforts and exertions," even though it neither breaches copyright nor constitutes plagiarism, so Goodman's definitions are inconsistent. McEwan's and Shaw's definitions are not specific enough. McEwan's does not distinguish plagiarism from other forms of intellectual dishonesty like forgery, nor does it indicate what conditions must be met for something to be "uniquely someone else's." Shaw's definition is insufficient because it is circular: How to tell when (or whether) plagiarism is wrongful is precisely the question.

Others have found it easier to ask what plagiarism is not. J. O. Urmson points out that, although theft is the most common analogy for plagiarism (witness the title I have used for this very chapter), it is not the best one. Theft typically involves "depriving permanently a living person of some object of value of which he is the owner without his consent." Breach of copyright may fit this description, but as Urmson points out (in contradiction to Goodman's claim, above, from the same symposium), "most breach of copyright does not involve plagiarism, and much plagiarism does not involve breach of copyright." Plagiarism surely does not deprive the plagiarized author of any fame or glory, so that is not being stolen. Nor is it the idea or the work that is being stolen, since stealing involves depriving the rightful owner of the stolen object, and the plagiarist does not so deprive the rightful owner of an idea or text.[1]

Ethical evaluation of plagiarism clearly needs to be considered in other terms than as an analogy with theft. The simpler analogue of deceit (which is behind, for instance, McEwan's definition above) is more satisfactory, but my earlier analysis of the creative author suggests that the analogue of deceit needs to be supplemented by another, pride, and also suggests why this is so. Of the five "functions" in creating a literary work (the ore, arché, archive, artisan, and artifact) the living writer of an original text will typically claim for himself or herself the role of artisan. But he will often claim responsibility for other roles as well, especially those of arché and archive. For example, I might tell the following story about my role in the creation of this book: While in a laudanum-induced reverie, I dreamed the entire manuscript, word for word, woke with perfect recall, and transcribed it precisely as you now are reading it, losing three chapters (which would have been the best ones) when a person from Porlock rang the doorbell. That story would not only claim for me the role of artisan, but also imply that my unconscious (a part of me), with assistance from an opiate, performed the function of the arché. By contrast, I might tell this story: After I had prayed and fasted forty days and forty nights, God, addressing me from a whirlwind, instructed me that it was time someone settled this author foolishness once and for all, and he handed me a pair of (large) stone tablets containing the very text you are now reading, with instructions to key it into my Macintosh and send it straight to Temple University Press. Such a story would limit my function strictly to that of artisan, and would attribute the functions of arché, archive, and so on, to entities other than myself. My telling the first story when the second was true would be plagiarism (taking credit for God's ideas as if they were my own), but my telling the second when the first was true, even though I would be intentionally deceiving anyone gullible enough to believe me, would not be plagiarism (since I would be *giving* credit falsely rather than *taking* it).

Plagiarism occurs when a writer claims for herself (explicitly or tacitly) more credit for the function of the arché than is actually due. Plagiarism, on this view, is wrong for the same reason it is wrong for the star of a basketball team to say in the locker room after the championship game of the Final Four that he is the only reason his team won. Such a statement would be an instance of deceit and hubris because, although it may be true that his team would not have won had he been injured or playing for the other team, it is not true that the other team members, the coaches, trainers, and so on, did not contribute to the victory. In other words, the star player's claim is false and proud for the simple reason that he did not win by himself but as a member of a team; he played only point guard, not center and power forward and coach and athletic director. The plagiarist does something similar. He claims to be playing more positions than he really is. If God really had dictated this text to me, and I claimed to have thought it all up myself, I would be guilty of deceit and pride; I would be guilty of plagiarism. If, on the other hand, the star player, on receiving the MVP award, gives the trophy to the school, saying that there are no stars on this team and that we won with a team effort under the guidance of our coach, then his statement, although it would be dishonest (since he is the most talented and hardest-working team member, without whom they would not have won), would be an instance of praiseworthy modesty. Similarly, if I had made up this text myself, but attributed it to God, I would be lying, but not plagiarizing. Deceit alone is not a sufficient condition for plagiarism.

The advantage of this view, that plagiarism consists in a writer's claiming for herself more credit for the function of the arché than is actually due, is that, unlike the definitions quoted above, it includes activities we intuitively consider plagiaristic and excludes those we do not. It includes, for instance, Posner's ghostwriting: The politician or columnist is taking credit for the arché's function, the origin of the ideas and words in the speech or column, but he or she did not actually perform that function. It excludes legitimate uses of "someone else's intellectual property," like documented quotation. Even the kind of allusion and quotation that occurs in poetry like Pound's *Cantos*, in which no effort is made to identify the source of every borrowed element, contains implicit and explicit disclaimers: Quotation marks or italics may be used to identify quoted material, and the insistence of the technique of juxtaposition itself functions as a sign that the writer is acknowledging the participation of others in performing the function of the arché.

More important, the view I am arguing for denies Bloom's claim that plagiarism is a necessary element of creativity, the claim from which he infers that the only condition under which plagiarism is wrong is when the borrowed material is poor in quality. Bloom's error, according to the view I am arguing for, is to mistake the ore for the arché. It is true that language, one portion of the ore for every literary work, has a history that makes it into a "web of allusion," and it is true that literature itself and writers themselves have histories that at least in part determine the ore available to them. The process of creation is in part a process of selection. But that the material from which the selection is made is allusive does not entail that the selection process, the selector, or the selected material is quotation. One can make an original sculpture out of lug nuts and radiators of junked automobiles. Although the ore is allusive, the archive need not be a quotation, so the function of the arché is not necessarily a plagiaristic one.

Consider the following instance. In *China Trace*, published in 1977, Charles Wright has two poems that apparently were prompted by, and certainly show the suffocating influence of, two earlier poems by W. S. Merwin. One of the Merwin poems is from *The Lice* (1967) and the other from *Writings to an Unfinished Accompaniment* (1973). Here is a poem by Wright followed by the first four lines of a poem from *The Lice*.

DEATH
I take you as I take the moon rising,
Darkness, black moth the light burns up in.

(122)

LOOKING EAST AT NIGHT
Death
White hand
The moths fly at in the darkness

216

I took you for the moon rising

(36)

If one removes the current title of the Merwin poem and
makes its first line into the title, virtually the only differences
left between the Wright poem and these lines of the Merwin
poem are two instances of what Freud's apparatus for dream
interpretation would call a "reversal": In Wright's poem the
moth wrestles with darkness instead of with light like the
moths in Merwin's poem, and in Wright's poem the moth wins
instead of losing like the moths in Merwin's poem. Or again:

JANUARY

In some other life
I'll stand where I'm standing now, and will look
    down, and will see
My own face, and not know what I'm looking at.

These are the nights
When the oyster begins her pearl, when the spi-
    der slips
Through his wired rooms, and the barns cough,
    and the grass quails.

(Wright 1982, 124)

EARLY ONE SUMMER

Years from now
someone will come upon a layer of birds
and not know what he is listening for

these are days
when the beetles hurry through dry grass
hiding pieces of light they have stolen

(Merwin 1973, 3)

Once more, the similarities overwhelm the superficial differences. Wright's poem is set early one winter instead of early one summer, and in some other life instead of years from now; in Wright's poem, the ignorance is visual instead of aural; and in Wright's poem the spider slips through his web at night instead of beetles hurrying through grass in the day. But the images, phrasing, and form are all similar, even down to the order in which they are presented.

Are these poems instances of plagiarism? If my definition is right, they are. But on what grounds? Neither "Death" nor "January" appears to be the result of conscious borrowing or conscious failure to acknowledge its source. Furthermore, since this is not a case of breach of copyright, since it is inadvertent rather than intentional, and on a very small scale, it is clearly not the sort of case that calls for legal action or imposition of the "draconian code" whose absence Shaw laments. Wright (unlike the high school student with the purchased term paper or the adult author who consciously takes another's work) is neither morally nor legally at fault. Yet there is something wrong, and curiously it is Bloom who comes closest to identifying what it is. He says that what is wrong with plagiarism has to do with the quality of the borrowed material; I suggest that what is wrong in this case has to do with quality and with the borrowed material, but not with the quality of the borrowed material. What is wrong with the borrowed material is that it has not yet become ore. A poem may become a part of the material from which new poems are created after its ways of using words have had time to sink into the language and its effects have had time to sink into the store of the literary community, but the transition from an artifact to ore is a gradual one. This is, I take it, what the laws concerning length of copyright protection attempt to capture, and why it is not a defense to say that Wright is alluding to Merwin's poems. Allusion is a legitimate enough literary technique, but it depends for its legitimacy as well as its success on the likelihood of recognition by a sufficient portion of the poet's intended audience, while plagiarism depends on lack of recognition (the only one of the two that could have been counted on in this case). Wright has used Merwin's two poems as archives, not as ore, a claim that might be explicated in a way straightforwardly connected with our intuitive notions about plagiarism: He uses them as archives, not as ore, because there is simply too little manipulation or alteration of the originals. They are not mere ingredients of the broth—they determine its flavor.

What is wrong concerning quality has to do with the quality not of the borrowed material but of the writer,[2] and it might be labeled "foreshortened influence." By this term I mean a historical nearsightedness of the sort that might be blamed for some of the impotence of much contemporary poetry. Foreshortened influence need not result in plagiarism: It occurs when, instead of learning from the past the immense variety available to and the originality demanded by greatness, poets study their contemporaries to learn the techniques suitable to a successful poem. Thus the poet's perspective on tradition becomes foreshortened, and he neglects Eliot's prophylaxis, to "procure the consciousness of the past and ... continue to develop this consciousness throughout his career" (40). In the instance I have cited, plagiarism is a sin of omission, not of commission; it arises not willfully, but through failure of will. The shirking of one responsibility (acquiring or making use of the historical consciousness from which great poetry arises) has led to the shirking of another.

No doubt the view I have put forward raises more problems and ambiguities about plagiarism than it solves. Certainly it does not give a solution to all cases a priori, eliminating the need for judgment. There are many gray areas left. But my aim has not been to settle once for all the issue of plagiarism, only to show that one who follows Barthes, Foucault, Bloom, and others in breaking from traditional conceptions of authorship like that of Hirsch (and even the now-traditional view espoused by Wimsatt and Beardsley) is not thereby committed to breaking with orthodox views about literary ethics, and need not renounce assessments of quality. I have tried to show in this chapter that the new view of authorship I have articulated in this book does not devalue literature and it does not (as deconstructionists like Bloom as well as opponents of deconstruction like William E. Cain, discussed in "Et Alii" above, have assumed any new view of authorship will) undermine the ethical and aesthetic imperatives of respect, singularity, honesty, and so on, that will attach themselves to and serve only something of immense worth.

CHAPTER 11

Our Vegetating Library

I n his introduction to the Hackett edition of Hume's *Dialogues Concerning Natural Religion*, Richard H. Popkin asks "who speaks for Hume in the Dialogues" (1980, xv), without recognizing that the *Dialogues* have put him in the same position in respect to Hume as the position of its characters in respect to God. Hume's characters wish to understand the Author of Nature by inference from nature. Popkin wishes to understand the author of the *Dialogues* by inference from them. Both efforts are futile.

The analogy between Popkin's position and that of Hume's characters should have become clear enough to Popkin from the *Dialogues*. Cleanthes specifically extends the argument from design, with which the characters are preoccupied throughout, to "our vegetating library" (25):

Suppose that there is a natural, universal, invariable language, common to every individual of human race, and that books are natural productions which perpetuate themselves in the same manner with animals and vegetables, by descent and propagation. . . . Suppose . . . that you enter into your library thus peopled by natural volumes containing the most refined reason and most exquisite beauty. Could you possibly open one of them and doubt that its original cause bore the strongest analogy to mind and intelligence? (24)

The same conclusion must hold for the reader of the text of nature and the reader of a written text: One must "assert either that a rational volume is no proof of a rational cause or admit of a similar cause to all the works of nature" (25). Both of the other interlocutors are struck by the force of the analogy. Philo is "a little embarrassed and confounded" (26), and Demea expands the analogy by emphasizing the Deity's incomprehensibility: "This volume of nature contains a great and inexplicable riddle, more than any intelligible discourse or reasoning" (26).

Unfortunately, as the rest of the *Dialogues* confirm, Demea is correct in asserting that the text of nature does not supply enough information for the characters to infer what they want to know; and neither does the text of the *Dialogues* supply the information Popkin wants to know. Philo looks to Popkin like the obvious choice for the character who "stands for" Hume himself, but at the last second Pamphilus declares Cleanthes the winner, with views "nearer to the truth" (89) than those of Philo. Popkin offers several possible explanations for the concluding remark of Pamphilus, none satisfying. What he misses is that Pamphilus's remark seals the analogy between this text and the text of nature: Neither will consent to be a transparent revelation of its author. By muddling the issue of which ideas "reveal" Hume himself, the *Dialogues* insure that in themselves, as in nature, no identity can be deduced between the author who originated the text and the author that can be inferred from it. There is no question whether God exists, only a question what he is like: "The question can never be concerning the *being* but only the *nature* of the Deity" (14); similarly, there is no question whether an author exists, only a question what the author is like.

If there is a conclusion upon which all parties agree at the end of the *Dialogues*, it is that natural religion and revealed religion alike end in theoretical aporia. But this failure or futility of theory, as all parties agree, leaves the practical necessities of nature and the moral imperatives of religion intact. Several of the writers whose work I have evaluated in this book have seized on the author/God analogy, and I can think of no better way to end a discourse on literary theory than by suggesting that the same is true of literature that Hume's characters hold true of the world. The failure of theory to produce a rational explanation of God's nature from the evidence of nature does not diminish the claims nature makes on us, and the failure of theory to produce an adequate explanation of the author from the evidence of texts does not diminish the claims literature makes on us.

Theory does not necessarily change that which it attempts to explain. One reason for the reluctance of past theorists to analyze the author has been the mistaken fear that the apparent diminution of the writer's importance that results when one examines the nature of authorship will weaken the text and diminish the power of literature, and to discard the "assumption of homogeneity," as this book advocates, appears at first to threaten the author's status. But to recognize that the author is neither singular nor homogeneous, that she is as much a fictional character as a physical human being, does not reduce her power or that of the text. As Pirandello reminds us, "A character, sir, may always ask a man who he is" (1952, 265). Even in theory, theory is not all that is at stake.

In the larger study of persons (of which one might say the study of authors is a part) theory has progressed beyond denials of multiplicity. If there is a historical focal point for this advance, it would be psychoanalysis. Descartes is a good example of the old "assumption of homogeneity" in persons: "I knew that I was a substance the whole essence or nature of which was merely to think, and which, in order to exist, needed no place and depended on no material thing. Thus, this 'I,' that is, the soul through which I am what I am, is entirely distinct from the body, . . . and even if there were no body, the soul would not cease to be all that it is" (1985, 18). Even though I *have* a body, I *am* a rational soul. There may be parts, but only one of them is authentic. Freud's discarding of the assumption of homogeneity, evident throughout his work, receives its most general formulation in the fourth of the *Introductory Lectures,* where he declares his aim to be the understanding of the mind as an interplay of opposing forces. The formulation most directly relevant to the problem of authorship comes in "On Narcissism," where he talks of the individual in terms reminiscent of the creative author/created author distinction I have tried to enforce in this book: "The individual does actually carry on a twofold existence: one to serve his own purposes and the other as a link in a chain, which he serves against his will, or at least involuntarily" (1959d, 78). Psychoanalysis begins by acknowledging that human beings are complex rather than simple, fragmentary rather than unitary. This change does not entail the sacrifice of human values, only a more pragmatic attitude toward how they are to be achieved. Freud does not desire human goodness any less than Descartes does, nor does he deny its possibility. He simply begins to seek goodness in terms of health instead of in terms of virtue. He aims to *achieve* unity (psychical health, for Freud, being achieved when what is unconscious is made conscious) instead of insisting that we must already *be* unitary.

That as persons we are multiple rather than unitary, heterogeneous rather than homogeneous, does not make us any less persons. In fact, it has been argued that multiplicity/heterogeneity is precisely the sine qua non of persons. Lynne McFall suggests that persons are "beings who have noninstrumental second-order volitions" (1989, 36).[1] That is, persons are beings who can entertain not only wishes but also wishes to revise their wishes. "For example, I want to want not to smoke, and I want this desire, rather than the desire to smoke, to be the one that is effective. This is a second-order volition" (37). On this view of persons, internal division or heterogeneity is not simply a fact about persons, but the condition of the possibility of personhood. W. B. Yeats puts into the terminology of masks what I take to be a similar idea: He suggests that a multiplicity of masks, rather than being an ethical downfall (as in the accusation that one is Janus-faced or two-faced), is the condition for ethical advancement. "If we cannot imagine ourselves as different from what we are, and try to assume that second self, we cannot impose a discipline upon ourselves though we may accept one from others. Active virtue, as distinguished from the passive acceptance of a code, is therefore theatrical, consciously dramatic, the wearing of a mask" (1969, 334).

The larger study of the production of meaning (another domain in which one might say the question of the author is located) has, like the study of persons, acknowledged the multiplicity/heterogeneity of its subject matter. From Aristotle's claims in the *Categories* ("expressions which are not in any way composite, such as 'man', 'white', 'runs', 'wins', cannot be either true or false" [2 a 9–10]) to the modern idea that a linguistic sign is a composite made of a signifier and a signified, language has been acknowledged to be a complex entity.

I have tried in this book to show that, like persons and language, the author is complex and heterogeneous. For too long now, interpretive formulae have treated the author as a constant; I have tried to show that the author is a variable. Until this is acknowledged, the results of interpretation cannot but be skewed. And the issue is too important to treat cursorily.

What is at stake in the theory of interpretation, after all, is how one encounters a text. And what is at stake when one encounters a text is not only who its author is, but who its reader is. The functioning of texts is often described as "play," but if reading and writing are games, the stakes are high, and the author is not the only one who risks his life. Interpretation is a complex struggle, and if a reconciliation is to be effected, it will not be a simple one. "The object of art," Wilde says, "is not simple truth but complex beauty" (1987, 917). In asking who the author is, I have tried not to ignore that complexity but to explore it. I have argued that theorists have been mistaken to defy the author's complexity, and I have tried as a corrective to begin to define it.

Notes, Works Cited, and Index

Notes

1. Vital Signs

1. From *Webster's New World Dictionary.* The word comes from the Greek *autopsia*, a seeing with one's own eyes.

2. Foucault says the author as we know him originated in the seventeenth and eighteenth centuries (1977, 125–26), Barthes traces the author back to "English empiricism, French rationalism and the personal faith of the Reformation" (1977, 142–43), and Nehamas cites Hobbes specifically (1987, 267ff.).

2. Foucault and Nehamas

1. Foucault should not be accused of overhasty generalizations on account of my summary: He *does* qualify his statements as being "far too categorical" (1977, 126).

2. Other, and far earlier, examples are easy to come by: Montaigne's essay "Various outcomes of the same plan" makes this point; and this point is one way to construe Socrates' complaint about the poets.

3. Agent is Nehamas's word, and the term "single" should not be taken to imply "simple" or "homogeneous." As I argue at length later, the created author (the "single agent" who is used to account for the presence and the meaning of a text's features) is a concatenation of forces working together.

4. This mistaken assumption that interpretation is analogous to scientific explanation helps to explain Nehamas's conflation, discussed above, of an author's accounting for the *presence* of a text's

features and his accounting for the *meaning* of those features. An *explanation* can account for the presence of a text's features, but only an *interpretation* can account for the meaning of those features.

3. *Barthes and Gass*

1. Polletta, in the paragraph from which I quote, is specifically comparing Barthes with Wimsatt and Beardsley. I have taken the liberty of applying his words to "most critics," since his insight seems to apply as well to Eliot, Frye, et al.

4. *Et Alii*

1. The allusion is to the e. e. cummings poem beginning "i sing of Olaf glad and big."

2. It is true that the terms are suggested by Walton's use of the label "apparent" author, but that does not excuse Stecker, who uses them throughout the essay, even when discussing Nehamas, who, as I mention, specifically draws attention to the need to avoid such terms.

5. *Five Modes of Creation*

1. In describing the modes, I speak as if the descriptions are accurate; that is, I say of the mythic mode that the arché gives the artisan a finished script as the archive. It is to be understood that I mean by that statement that what is claimed for the work or said about the work, when translated into my conceptual schema, is that the arché gives the artisan a finished script. I am no more concerned with the issue of whether or not the arché exists as a real, separate entity than I am concerned with whether Hamlet was really Prince of Denmark when evaluating his power of action in Shakespeare's play in the light of Frye's fictional modes.

2. That it is precisely these two functions that are at issue in poetry's exile from the ideal state is explicit in the *Republic* in passages like this one in Book 10 (607c–e), after poetry has been banished for

its inability to teach: "But nevertheless let it be declared that, if the mimetic and dulcet poetry can show any reason for her existence in a well-governed state, we would gladly admit her, since we ourselves are very conscious of her spell. . . . And we shall listen [to a defense of poetry by her advocates] benevolently, for it will be clear gain for us if it can be shown that she bestows *not only pleasure but benefit*" (my emphasis).

3. It should be noted that Rorty takes great pains to show that the modern conception of the "mind" is different from the ancient conception, and that Rorty's central concern is with the modern conception; and further, that Rorty, although he does not cite this particular passage in Plato, does trace the roots of even the modern conception of the mind back to Platonism. So I am *not* suggesting that Rorty "missed one."

6. *Creative Dynamics*

1. Two observations about the procreative metaphor might be added. First, that the procreative metaphor is not without relation to the modes outlined in the previous chapter. Notice, for instance, that with the shift to the empirical mode, in which the ore usurps the function of the arché and diminishes or negates the importance of the artisan, comes an increased use of paternal metaphors, so that a writer like Jacques Derrida eschews Frye's masculine/feminine distinction for an almost exclusive use of masculine metaphors: onanism, dissemination, and so on.

Second, that reading has been based throughout Western culture on the use of the procreative metaphor for artistic creation. The traditional notion of reading is among the results of our patriarchal culture. Consider this statement from one of Freud's case histories: "A great advance was made in civilization when men decided to put their inferences upon a level with the testimony of their senses and to make the step from matriarchy to patriarchy.—The prehistoric figures which show a smaller person sitting upon the head of a larger one are representations of patrilineal descent; Athena had no mother, but sprang from the head of Zeus. A witness who testifies to something before a court of law is still called *'Zeuge'* [literally, "begetter"] in German, after the part played by the male in the act of procreation; so too in hieroglyphics a 'witness' is represented pictorially by the male genitals" (1959c, 368–69). If I am right to say that the act of writing poetry traditionally has been thought of, on analogy with the act of procreation, as the arché impregnating the artisan with the archive, then it seems fair to say that the act of interpreting literature traditionally has been a correlative of the switch, identified here by Freud, from the matriarchal testimony of the senses to the patriarchal inference. That is, literature is usually thought of as writing that has a surface meaning and also a deeper, more or less hidden meaning. And the task of the critic has been seen as that of inferring, "behind" the maternal "sense testimony" of the surface meaning (the words of the artisan; the artifact), the deeper paternal, "true" meaning of the text (the words, idea, or meaning of the arché; the archive).

2. Much of the story is left out of this quotation; for Justice's full account, see *Platonic Scripts*, 55–57 and 25–27.

3. It is important to point out that the following account of displacement assumes without argument that the artifact mentioned is the artifact at the reader's disposal, which may or may not be identical to that which the artisan's hands immediately produced. The sophomore reading "The Waste Land" in her *Norton Anthology* may be reading the same words, but is not reading the same *thing*, Eliot typed. That the two (that which the artisan immediately produced and that which is at the reader's disposal) may not be identical is what lends to original paintings their great monetary value and what keeps textual critics busy. The questions of where the "text" is, where the "meaning" is, and so on, will be addressed more directly in my discussion of the created author.

4. My inclusion of translation as a phenomenon of authorship in the same class as the reproduction of a book by a scribe or publisher may seem curious enough to require a defense. I have mentioned above that the artifact whose creation I hope to explain is the artifact available to the reader. This artifact in the case of literature will usually

be in printed rather than holograph form, and it will sometimes be in translation. Common literary and bibliographic practice also supports the inclusion of translation as a form of displacement. We are in the habit of referring to works in translation as having been written by (for example) Plato and translated by F. M. Cornford; we speak, that is, of Plato rather than Cornford as the author of even the English translation of the *Timaeus*, and include that translation as one node in the continuous history of a single work. Translations, after all, are works of art, too; and a complete exposition of artistic creation must account for translation or else defend itself against the charge of inconsistency on account of the arbitrary exclusion of one form of art commonly thought of as continuous with forms that the exposition does try to explain.

5. There are a number of questions that might be associated with cases of displacement and multiplication (for example: How does one tell when two artifacts, say the "Prototractatus" and the *Tractatus*, are variants of a single artifact and when they are different works?), but that I will not attempt to answer, on the grounds that my discussions of displacement and multiplication do not directly contribute anything toward an answer to those particular questions.

7. *The Implied Author*

1. The phrases in quotation marks are Booth's references to Hume's description of the ideal reader in "The Standard of Taste."

2. A series of such questions is discussed at length in Michel Foucault's *The Archaeology of Knowledge*. Foucault sets himself as a preliminary task to suspend the discursive unities "that emerge in the most immediate way: those of the book and the *œuvre*" (1982, 23).

3. Not only the existentialists, of course, but a long tradition of thinkers would question Robinson's assumption that the character of an action is determined by the character of the agent. One might appeal, for example, to Aristotle, who argues in the *Nichomachean Ethics* that a man's action may be just or temperate without the man himself being just or temperate; and that men are not by nature just or temperate, but only become so by doing just or temperate things.

8. *The Created Author*

1. Whether the reader and the artifact are homogeneous or whether they stand in need of the same kind of analysis to which this book attempts to subject the author is an important issue. In fact, I think they *do* need such an analysis, and the lack of one has already forced compromise in the section on displacement in an earlier chapter; but I will not attempt to provide an analysis for either artifact or reader here.

2. Even this is an oversimplification, since simple misreading as well as phenomena like dyslexia and illiteracy attest to the assumption of a certain minimal "competence" (to borrow from Chomsky) on the part of the reader, but it is an oversimplification that for the purposes of this chapter may be ignored.

3. It is not yet necessary to distinguish between the two proxies, though such a distinction will be made shortly. The important distinction at this point is between the narrator within the text and a proxy thought of as more or less "outside of" the text. In fact, a rudimentary account of schizoscription could be made without ever distinguishing the two proxies. William E. Tolhurst does something like this in a discussion of intention using *A Modest Proposal* as an example, explaining irony as "often the result of a discrepancy or tension between the meaning of the word sequence and the meaning of the utterance" (1979, 6), where an utterance is a token of the typical word sequence, so that irony results in the sentence "Nixon is the best president since Lincoln" when the meaning of the utterance (that Nixon is not a good president at all) is different from the meaning of the word sequence (that Nixon is a very good president) (1979, 4). The central difference is that schizoscription captures the element of personality associated with agents whose intention is irony.

4. My justification for pitting Zimmerman's discussion of irony against Frye's discussion of satire is that Zimmerman's concern in these passages is the irony in Swift, while satire for Frye is the type of irony that Swift makes use of. Both irony and satire operate by satirical schizoscription, whether one follows Frye's or Zimmerman's use of the terms.

5. Interestingly, Francis Sparshott makes a very similar distinction in "The Case of the Unreliable Author." He says that "the authorial presence may make itself felt in at least three distinct ways: as a distinctive voice through which a personalized writer is projected for what is written; as a manipulating intelligence sensed as ventriloquially skewing a narrator's supposedly integral version of events; or, colorlessly, as the writerly intelligence postulated when we accord to a set of marks the status of a written text" (1986, 162).

6. This is the reason I say above that the figurative corresponds roughly to the divine view; the literal always corresponds to the human view, but the figurative corresponds to the divine view just in case the two views differ. The literal and the figurative for Augustine are, of course, not mutually exclusive; one locution may have both a literal and a figurative meaning.

7. In Augustine on Scripture, the singular proxy's intention (that of the writer of the passage) is roughly the same as the narrator's. Like the narrator's intention, whether the singular proxy's intention coincides with that of the synoptic proxy (God) depends on whether the passage is literal or figurative.

8. From Kaufmann's footnote on p. 15.

9. This should serve as a reminder that, like the other terms introduced in these two chapters, the synoptic proxy and the singular proxy are not fixed, but variable; they are differential entities in Saussure's sense. For instance, one might have occasion to speak of a comparison between the Shakespeare of the great tragedies alone and the Shakespeare of the entire corpus. In such a case, "the Shakespeare of the great tragedies" would be functioning as the singular proxy and "the Shakespeare of the entire corpus" as the synoptic proxy. On the other hand, if one were trying to demonstrate the uniqueness of *King Lear*, one might speak of the Shakespeare of *Lear* versus the Shakespeare of the other great tragedies. In that case, "the Shakespeare of *Lear*" would be functioning as the singular proxy and "the Shakespeare of the other great tragedies" as the synoptic proxy. In a sense, then, what defines the singular proxy and the synoptic proxy is not so much their relationships with the works in question, but the relationship between themselves. The singular proxy is what the synoptic proxy is not, and vice versa.

10. Francis Murphy points out that, though "admirers often prefer the first edition of 1855 or the edition of 1860," still "no one . . . has seriously suggested publishing either the edition of 1855 or 1860 as a substitute for the last" (Whitman 1975, 21).

11. This is Charles H. Kahn's translation, except that I have retained the word *logos*. Unless otherwise noted, all translations will be Kahn's, with any modifications in brackets. In quoted passages, I have silently substituted transliterations for Greek words.

12. Kirk 1954, 204. The quoted material is Kirk's summary of Zeller's argument, not Zeller's own words.

13. Marcovich and Kahn each makes his own numbering system, but for the sake of uniformity I will follow (like Kirk) the numbers in Diels and Kranz. Marcovich translates fragment 80 this way: "One must know that war is common and strife is justice and that all things come to pass by strife and necessity" (1967, 137).

14. Dennis Dutton has made a similar observation in describing what he calls "stepping into the wrong [hermeneutic] circle" (1987, 201). Illustrating his claim by an anthropologist's misunderstanding of Hopi pottery, Dutton says that "once you have stepped into the wrong hermeneutic circle, there may come to light no obvious evidence to help you overcome your mistake" (201). The interpreter's initial hypothesis about meaning may support itself, even though it is not the best hypothesis.

15. In that case, the range of possibilities will naturally be wide; in the case of a freshman reading his first Elizabethan drama, perhaps no more specific than negative notions such as the improbability by virtue of his dates that Shakespeare will have written about space travel. For a more experienced reader encountering *Timon of Athens* for the first time after having read several of Shakespeare's other plays, the set of limits imposed by the synoptic proxy will be much narrower. Borrowing from John Connolly's Wittgensteinian reading of Gadamer in "Gadamer and the Author's Authority: a Language-Game Approach," one might say that to a reader unfamiliar with a particular work and unfamiliar with the writer of that work, the limits of the proxy are roughly the same as those of the language-game the reader is playing.

9. *The Book with a Shattered Author*

1. For Derrida on the inside versus the outside, see, for instance, the section "The Outside Is the Inside" in *Of Grammatology* (1976, 44–65), or "Outwork" in *Dissemination* (1981, 1–59). While Derrida is concerned with "exteriority" and concepts related to it, like "supplementarity," I argue here and in the earlier chapter on Derrida that in his conception of the author he has not escaped the traditional order of subordination in the hierarchy inside/outside.

10. *"Hiding Pieces of Light They Have Stolen"*

1. Michael Wreen agrees, offering the same justification Urmson gives, but expanding it to include other forms of "artistic crime," specifically forgery and piracy.

2. My claim of poor quality on the part of the writer as regards these two poems is not a general claim about Charles Wright any more than would be a criticism of the poems on other grounds. It would be a mistake (an instance of poor quality on his part) for Wright to publish unfinished poems or juvenilia, but that would not destroy him as a poet or the rest of his work. In fact, while I believe these two poems would have been better left out of the canon, I admire much of Wright's work, notably his very fine "Homage to Paul Cézanne" from *The Southern Cross.*

11. *Our Vegetating Library*

1. "The source of this suggestion," says McFall, is Harry Frankfurt, "Freedom of the Will and the Concept of a Person," *The Journal of Philosophy* 68 (1971): 5–20, as reprinted in Joel Feinberg, ed., *Reason and Responsibility*, 4th ed. (Encino and Belmont, CA: Dickenson Publ. Co., 1975), 395–403.

Works Cited

Anselm, St. 1965. *Proslogion*. Trans. M. J. Charlesworth. Oxford: Oxford University Press .

Aristotle. 1941a. *Categories*. In *The Basic Works of Aristotle*. Ed. Richard McKeon. New York: Random House. 3–37.

———. 1941b. *Metaphysics*. In *The Basic Works*. 681–926.

Augustine, St. 1980. *On Christian Doctrine*. Trans. D. W. Robertson, Jr. Indianapolis: Bobbs-Merrill.

Bagwell, J. Timothy. 1986. *American Formalism and the Problem of Interpretation*. Houston: Rice University Press.

Bally, Charles, and Albert Sechehaye. 1966. Preface to the First Edition. In Saussure 1966, xvii–xx.

Barthes, Roland. 1977. "The Death of the Author." In *Image—Music—Text*. Trans. Stephen Heath. New York: Hill and Wang. 142–48.

Bloom, Harold, et al. 1982. "Plagiarism—a symposium." *Times Literary Supplement* 9 April (4123): 413–15.

Booth, Wayne C. 1961. *The Rhetoric of Fiction*. Chicago: University of Chicago Press.

Bowra, C. M. 1952. *Heroic Poetry*. London: Macmillan.

Brooks, Cleanth, John Thibaut Purser, and Robert Penn Warren. 1975. *An Approach to Literature*. 5th ed. Englewood Cliffs: Prentice-Hall.

Burke, Kenneth. 1969. *A Grammar of Motives*. Berkeley: University of California Press.

Cain, William E. 1980. "Authors and Authority in Interpretation." *Georgia Review* 34.3 (Fall): 617–34.

Works Cited

Carpenter, Rhys. 1933. "The Antiquity of the Greek Alphabet." *American Journal of Archaeology* 37.1 (Jan.–March): 8–29.

Cherniss, Harold. 1935. *Aristotle's Criticism of Presocratic Philosophy.* Baltimore: Johns Hopkins University Press.

Connolly, John. 1986. "Gadamer and the Author's Authority: A Language-Game Approach." *The Journal of Aesthetics and Art Criticism* 44.3 (Spring): 271–77.

Culler, Jonathan. 1975. *Structuralist Poetics: Structuralism, Linguistics, and the Study of Literature.* Ithaca: Cornell University Press.

——. 1977. *Ferdinand de Saussure.* New York: Penguin.

——. 1983. *Roland Barthes.* New York: Oxford University Press.

Davison, J. A. 1955. "Peisistratus and Homer." *Transactions of the American Philological Association* 86: 1–21.

Derrida, Jacques. 1972. "Signature Event Context." In *Margins of Philosophy.* Trans. Alan Bass. Chicago: University of Chicago Press. 307–30.

——. 1976. *Of Grammatology.* Trans. Gayatri Chakravorty Spivak. Baltimore: Johns Hopkins University Press.

——. 1981. *Dissemination.* Trans. Barbara Johnson. Chicago: University of Chicago Press.

——. 1986. "Interpreting Signatures (Nietzsche/Heidegger): Two Questions." Trans. Diane Michelfelder and Richard E. Palmer. *Philosophy and Literature* 10.2 (Oct.): 246–62.

Descartes, René. 1985. *Discourse on Method and Meditations on First Philosophy.* Trans. Donald A. Cress. Indianapolis: Hackett.

Donnellan, Keith S. 1977. "Speaking of Nothing." In *Naming, Necessity, and Natural Kinds.* Ed. Stephen P. Schwartz. Ithaca: Cornell University Press. 216–44.

Dutton, Dennis. 1987. "Why Intentionalism Won't Go Away." In *Literature and the Question of Philosophy.* Ed. Anthony J. Cascardi. Baltimore: Johns Hopkins University Press. 194–209.

Eadmer. 1972. *The Life of St. Anselm.* Ed. and trans. R. W. Southern. Oxford: Oxford University Press.

Eliot, T. S. 1975. "Tradition and the Individual Talent." In *Selected Prose of T. S. Eliot.* Ed. Frank Kermode. New York: Harcourt Brace Jovanovich. 37–44.

Works Cited

Emerson, Ralph Waldo. 1968. "Self-Reliance." In *Ralph Waldo Emerson: Essays and Journals*. Ed. Lewis Mumford. Garden City, NY: Doubleday.

Finlay, John. 1986. "The Graves by the Sea." Trans. of Paul Valéry, "Le Cimetière Marin." *The Southern Review* 22.1 (Winter): 118–22.

Flacelière, Robert. 1965. *Greek Oracles*. Trans. Douglas Garman. London: Elek.

Foucault, Michel. 1977. "What Is an Author?" In *Language, Counter-Memory, Practice: Selected Essays and Interviews*. Ed. Donald F. Bouchard. Trans. Bouchard and Sherry Simon. Ithaca: Cornell University Press. 113–38.

———. 1982. *The Archaeology of Knowledge*. Trans. A. M. Sheridan Smith. New York: Pantheon.

Frank, Erich. 1982. *Philosophical Understanding and Religious Truth*. Lanham, MD: University Press of America.

Freud, Sigmund. 1959a. *An Autobiographical Study*. In *The Standard Edition of the Complete Psychological Works of Sigmund Freud* 20. London: Hogarth.

———. 1959b. *Leonardo da Vinci and a Memory of His Childhood*. In *The Standard Edition* 11.

———. 1959c. "Notes Upon a Case of Obsessional Neurosis." In *Collected Papers* 3. New York: Basic Books. 291–383.

———. 1959d. "On Narcissism." In *The Standard Edition* 14.

———. 1959e. "The Uncanny." In *The Standard Edition* 17.

Frye, Northrop. 1957. *Anatomy of Criticism: Four Essays*. Princeton: Princeton University Press.

Gadamer, Hans-Georg. 1975. *Truth and Method*. New York: Crossroad.

———. 1980. "Plato and the Poets." In *Dialogue and Dialectic*. Trans. P. Christopher Smith. New Haven: Yale University Press. 39–72.

Gass, William. 1986a. "The Death of the Author." In *Habitations of the Word*. New York: Simon and Schuster. 265–88.

———. 1986b. "The Soul Inside the Sentence." In *Habitations of the Word*. 113–40.

Goodman, Lord. 1982. In Bloom 1982, 413.

Grene, David. 1967. Introduction. In Samuel Butler, *The Authoress of the Odyssey.* Chicago: University of Chicago Press.

Havelock, Eric A. 1963. *Preface to Plato.* Cambridge: Harvard University Press.

Hegel, G. W. F. 1977. *Phenomenology of Spirit.* Trans. A. V. Miller. London: Oxford University Press.

Hemingway, Ernest. 1987. "I Guess Everything Reminds You of Something." In *The Complete Short Stories of Ernest Hemingway.* New York: Charles Scribner's Sons.

Hirsch, E. D., Jr. 1967. *Validity in Interpretation.* New Haven: Yale University Press.

Hobbes, Thomas. 1984. *Leviathan.* Ed. C. B. Macpherson. New York: Penguin.

Homer. 1961. *The Iliad.* Trans. Richmond Lattimore. Chicago: University of Chicago Press.

Hughes, Merritt Y. 1957. Note on *Areopagitica.* In Milton 1957, 716–17.

Hume, David. 1980. *Dialogues Concerning Natural Religion.* Ed. Richard H. Popkin. Indianapolis: Hackett.

Jeffery, L. H. 1961. *The Local Scripts of Archaic Greece.* London: Oxford University Press.

Johnson, Barbara. 1981. Translator's Introduction. In Derrida 1981, vii-xxxiii.

Jung, C. G. 1933. "Psychology and Literature." In *Modern Man in Search of a Soul.* Trans. W. S. Dell and Cary F. Baynes. New York: Harcourt Brace Jovanovich. 152–72.

Justice, Donald. 1984. *Platonic Scripts.* Ann Arbor: University of Michigan Press.

Kahn, Charles H. 1979. *The Art and Thought of Heraclitus.* Cambridge: Cambridge University Press.

Keats, John. 1977. *The Complete Poems.* Ed. John Barnard. New York: Penguin.

Kirk, G. S. 1954. *Heraclitus: The Cosmic Fragments.* Cambridge: Cambridge University Press.

———. 1962. *The Songs of Homer.* Cambridge: Cambridge University Press.

————. 1979. "Homer and Modern Oral Poetry: Some Confusions." In Latacz 1979, 320–37.

Kronman, Anthony. 1980. "The Concept of an Author and the Unity of the Commonwealth in Hobbes's *Leviathan*." *Journal of the History of Philosophy* 18.2 (April): 159–75.

Latacz, Joachim. 1979. *Homer: Tradition und Neuerung*. Darmstadt: Wissenschaftliche Buchgesellschaft.

Lindsell, Harold. 1976. *The Battle for the Bible*. Grand Rapids: Zondervan.

Lord, Albert. 1979. "Homer's Originality: Oral Dictated Texts." In Latacz 1979, 308–19.

Lorimer, H. L. 1950. *Homer and the Monuments*. London: Macmillan.

Luria, A. R. 1973. *The Working Brain: An Introduction to Neuropsychology*. Trans. Basil Haigh. New York: Basic.

————. 1987. *The Man with a Shattered World*. Trans. Lynn Solotaroff. Cambridge: Harvard University Press.

McEwan, Ian. 1982. In Bloom 1982, 413–14.

McFall, Lynne. 1987. "Integrity." *Ethics* 98 (Oct.): 5–20.

————. 1989. *Happiness*. New York: Peter Lang.

Mackey, Louis. 1971. *Kierkegaard: A Kind of Poet*. Philadelphia: University of Pennsylvania Press.

Marcovich, Miroslav. 1967. *Heraclitus: A Greek Text with a Short Commentary*. Merida, Venezuela: Los Andes University Press.

Merwin, W. S. 1967. *The Lice*. New York: Atheneum.

————. 1973. *Writings to an Unfinished Accompaniment*. New York: Atheneum.

Milton, John. 1957. *Complete Poems and Major Prose*. Ed. Merritt Y. Hughes. Indianapolis: Odyssey.

Murray, Penelope. 1981. "Poetic Inspiration in Early Greece." *Journal of the Hellenic Society* 101: 87–100.

Myers, F. W. H. 1911. *Essays: Classical*. London: Macmillan.

Nehamas, Alexander. 1981. "The Postulated Author: Critical Monism as a Regulative Ideal." *Critical Inquiry* 8.1 (Autumn): 133–49.

————. 1986. "What an Author Is." *The Journal of Philosophy* 83.11 (Nov.): 685–91.

————. 1978. "Writer, Text, Work, Author." In *Literature and the*

Question of Philosophy. Ed. Anthony J. Cascardi. Baltimore: Johns Hopkins University Press. 267–91.

Nietzsche, Friedrich. 1968. *The Birth of Tragedy.* In *Basic Writings of Nietzsche.* Trans. and ed. Walter Kaufmann. New York: Modern Library. 15–144.

Olson, Charles. 1983. *The Maximus Poems.* Ed. George F. Butterick. Berkeley: University of California Press.

Page, D. L. 1956. "Greek Vases from the Eighth Century B.C." *The Classical Review* N.S. 6: 95–97.

Paley, William. 1854. *Natural Theology.* In *The Works of William Paley.* Philadelphia: Crissy and Markley.

Parke, H. W. 1967. *Greek Oracles.* London: Hutchinson University Library.

Parry, Milman. 1980. *The Making of Homeric Verse.* Ed. Adam Parry. New York: Arno.

Pirandello, Luigi. 1952. *Six Characters in Search of an Author.* In *Naked Masks.* Ed. Eric Bentley. New York: E. P. Dutton. 209–76.

Plato. 1961. *The Collected Dialogues of Plato.* Ed. Edith Hamilton and Huntington Cairns. Princeton: Princeton University Press.

Polletta, Gregory T. 1984. "The Author's Place in Contemporary Narratology." In *Contemporary Approaches to Narrative.* Ed. Anthony Mortimer. Tubingen: Narr. 109–23.

Posner, Ari. 1988. "Reams and Reams of Plagiarism." *Kansas City Star & Times* 24 April, Sun.: 1-I, 6-I. Reprinted from *The New Republic.*

Robinson, Jenefer M. 1985. "Style and Personality in the Literary Work." *The Philosophical Review* 94.2 (April): 227–47.

Rorty, Richard. 1980. *Philosophy and the Mirror of Nature.* Princeton: Princeton University Press.

Saussure, Ferdinand de. 1966. *Course in General Linguistics.* Ed. Charles Bally and Albert Sechehaye. Trans. Wade Baskin. New York: McGraw-Hill.

Shakespeare, William. 1980. *The Complete Works of Shakespeare.* 3rd ed. Ed. David Bevington. Glenview, IL: Scott, Foresman.

Shaw, Peter. 1982. "Plagiary." *The American Scholar* 51.3 (Summer): 325–37.

Works Cited

Sparshott, Francis. 1986. "The Case of the Unreliable Author." *Philosophy and Literature* 10.2 (Oct.): 145–67.

Sperduti, Alice. 1950. "The Divine Nature of Poetry in Antiquity." *Transactions of the American Philological Association* 81: 209–40.

Stecker, Robert. 1987. "Apparent, Implied, and Postulated Authors." *Philosophy and Literature* 11.2 (Oct.): 258–71.

Stevens, Wallace. 1981. *The Necessary Angel: Essays on Reality and the Imagination.* New York: Vintage.

Strand, Mark. 1982. "Notes on the Craft of Poetry." In *Claims for Poetry.* Ed. Donald Hall. Ann Arbor: University of Michigan Press.

Tigerstedt, E. N. 1970. "*Furor Poeticus:* Poetic Inspiration in Greek Literature before Democritus and Plato." *Journal of the History of Ideas* 31.2 (April–June): 163–78.

Tolhurst, William E. 1979. "On What a Text Is and How It Means." *The British Journal of Aesthetics* 19.1 (Winter): 3–14.

Urmson, J. O. 1982. In Bloom 1982, 415.

Valéry, Paul. 1971. *Le Cimetière Marin.* Ed. and trans. Graham Dunstan Martin. Austin: University of Texas Press.

Whitman, Cedric H. 1965. *Homer and the Heroic Tradition.* New York: Norton.

Whitman, Walt. 1975. *The Complete Poems.* Ed. Francis Murphy. New York: Penguin.

Wilde, Oscar. 1987. "The Decay of Lying." In *The Works of Oscar Wilde.* Leicester: Galley Press. 909–31.

Wittgenstein, Ludwig. 1961. *Tractatus Logico-Philosophicus.* Trans. D. F. Pears and B. F. McGuinness. London: Routledge and Kegan Paul.

Wordsworth, William. 1932. "Preface to the Second Edition of Several of the Foregoing Poems, &c." In *The Poetical Works of Wordsworth.* Ed. Thomas Hutchinson. London: Oxford University Press. 934–42.

Wreen, Michael. 1984. "Some Remarks on Forgery, Plagiarism, and Piracy." *The Southern Journal of Philosophy* 22.1 (Spring): 129–37.

Works Cited

Wright, Charles. 1982. *Country Music: Selected Early Poems.* Middletown, CT: Wesleyan University Press.

Yeats, William Butler. 1969. *Per Amica Silentia Lunae.* In *Mythologies.* New York: Collier. 317–69.

Zimmerman, Everett. 1983. *Swift's Narrative Satires: Author and Authority.* Ithaca: Cornell University Press.

Index

Index

Consciousness, 48–49

Consistency, 156–157. *See also* Style

Context, 76

Corngold, Stanley, 36

Created author, 39, 158, 162–163. *See also* Creative author; Implied author; Narrator; Proxy

Creation, 57, 81; according to Freud, 102–104; compared to production, preservation, 58–59, 134; methods of, 62, 118–119; of Homeric poems, 134–140; relation to gender, 116–117; relation to plagiarism, 215–216. *See also* Creative author; Modes, creative

Creative author, 39, 143, 158, 162; relation to proxy, 169, 183. *See also* Agent; Arché; Artisan; Created author

Criticism, 35, 183

Culler, Jonathan, 104–106, 132

Darwin, Charles, 68–69

Davison, J. A., 137

Death: of the author, 3, 6, 41–60, 77; of God, 3, 47–48; kinship with writing, 17, 205. *See also* Birth

Deceit, 213–216. *See also* Plagiarism

Deconstruction, 27, 32, 34, 198. *See also* Derrida, Jacques

Derrida, Jacques, 75–78, 197–199. *See also* Deconstruction

Descartes, 223–224

Deuteronomy. *See* Ten Commandments

Diodorus Siculus, 91

Discourse, 64–65

Discursive practice, initiators of, 23–24

Displacement, 120–128; definition of, 120; in Homer, 139. *See also* Accidental displacement; Limited displacement; Systematic displacement

Divination, Greek, 91–92

Donnellan, Keith S., 19–20

Double, the, 17

Dreams, as similar to artistic creation, 103

Eadmer, 97–99

Ecriture, 18

Eliot, T. S., 43, 219

Emerson, Ralph Waldo, 184

Empirical mode, 104–106; definition of, 88; in Plato, 110, 112–113. *See also* Modes, creative

Epic, Greek, 17

Exodus. *See* Ten Commandments

Explanation, 36. *See also* Interpretation

Expression: of personality, 154–157; ambiguity of term, 158–160; by Zasetsky, 206. *See also* Style

Figurative language, 172–173

Finlay, John, 125

Flacelière, Robert, 91

Flaubert, Gustave, 147, 152–153

Proxy privilege, 176–185
Proxy revision, 185–193
Pseudonyms, 50–51, 182–183

Reader, 39, 111–113, 192–193;
constructs author, 38, 144–
145, 186; in schizoscription,
165, 168, 171; obligations of,
28; power of, 46–47, 52, 54,
63, 165; relation to created
author, 149–151, 164, 170; relation to writer, 38, 204–205.
See also Author, political implications of; Created author
Reading, "apostolic" method of,
174
Real mode, 102–104, 126, 138;
definition of, 88. *See also*
Modes, creative
Reality: of created author, 72–
73; of intentions, 74; vs. appearance in Plato, 110–113
Reliability of text, 130
Representation in Plato, 110–
113
Resonance. *See* Kahn, Charles
H.
Responsibility: for narrative,
42–43; of author and reader,
65, 69–70, 158, 219. *See also*
Author, ethical implications
of
Revisionism, 27
Rights, 4–5; of authors, 50. *See
also* Author, political implica-
tions of
Robinson, Jenefer M., 153–162
Rorty, Richard, 110

Satire. *See* Satirical schiz-
oscription
Satirical schizoscription, 165–
171. *See also* Allegorical
schizoscription; Schiz-
oscription
Saussure, Ferdinand de, 82, 123–
124, 131–132
Schizoscription, 165–176. *See
also* Allegorical schizoscrip-
tion; Satirical schizoscription
Scriptor. *See* Barthes, Roland;
Writer
Searle, John, 19
Shaw, Peter, 210–213
Signature, 52, 75–78
Signs, 16, 92, 172. *See also* Lan-
guage
Simple multiplication, 129–131.
See also Complex multiplica-
tion; Multiplication
Singular proxy: definition of,
164; in satirical schizoscrip-
tion, 168–169; relation to nar-
rator and synoptic proxy, 169–
171. *See also* Proxy
Singular proxy privilege, 178–
185
Socrates. *See* Plato
Sound, 82, 124–125
Stecker, Robert, 71–75
Stevens, Wallace, 62, 124
Structuralism, 27, 32, 104–106
Style, 51, 153–162
Subject: as a function of dis-
course, 24; Cartesian, 71–72;
disappearance of, 17, 42;
transformation of, 45. *See also*
Agent